Henry Moorhouse: The English Evangelist

Collective Writings and Sermons
of Henry Moorhouse

Henry Moorhouse: The English Evangelist

Entered according to the Act of Congress in the year of 1881, by F. H. Revell, in the Office of Librarian of Congress at Washington, D.C.

HENRY MOORHOUSE: THE ENGLISH EVANGELIST
Collective Writings and Sermons of Henry Moorhouse
By: Henry Moorhouse

Copyright © 2010
GOSPEL FOLIO PRESS
All Rights Reserved

Published by
GOSPEL FOLIO PRESS
304 Killaly St. W.
Port Colborne, ON L3K 6A6
CANADA

ISBN: 9781926765273

Cover design by Lisa Martin

All Scripture quotations from the
King James Version unless otherwise noted.

Printed in USA

Contents

Foreword

The Man Who Loved John 3:16

"For God so loved the world, that He gave His only begotten Son, that whosoever believeth in Him should not perish, but have everlasting life" (John 3:16).

Henry Moorhouse was a wild young man who, by the age sixteen, was a gambler, gang-leader, and thief. But during the Revival of 1859, Henry gave his life to Jesus. He was soon heard preaching the Gospel with all his heart; and his favourite text was John 3:16. One day in Ireland in 1867, he met the far-famed evangelist, D. L. Moody; and Henry had the nerve to invite himself to preach in Moody's church in Chicago.

Sometime later, Moody returned home from a trip and learned that Moorhouse had shown up, started preaching, and was drawing great crowds. "He has preached two sermons from John 3:16," Moody's wife said to him, "and I think you will like him, although he preached a little different from what you do."

"How is that?"

"Well, he tells sinners God loves them."

Moody wasn't too sure about that; but that evening he went to hear Moorhouse preach. The young man stood up in the pulpit and said, "If you will turn to the third chapter of John and the sixteenth verse," said the young man, "you will find my text." Moody later recalled, "He preached a most extraordinary sermon from that verse... I never knew up to that time that God loved us so much. This heart of mine began to thaw out, and I could not keep back the tears. It was like news from a far country. I just drank it in."

Night after night, Moorhouse preached from John 3:16, and it had a life-changing effect on D. L. Moody. "I never forgotten those nights," Moody said later. "I have preached a different Gospel since, and I have had more power with God and man since then."

Later, when Moorhouse fell ill and was on his deathbed, he looked up and told his friends, "If it were the Lord's will to raise me again, I should like to preach from the text, 'God so loved the world.'"

—Robert J. Morgan

September 22, 2009.

Ruth the Moabitess

Chapter 1
Ruth Deciding

I suppose our friends have noticed that there are in the Bible a great many striking pictures of the way in which God is dealing with Israel and with His Church at the present time.

I want you to understand definitely, once for all, that I do not say these pictures we are going to look at are types, or that God intended them for types: because I should be sorry to take anything out of the Old Testament and say it was a type, or that God intended it for a type, if I were not positive from the New Testament that it were so. But there are certainly wonderful lessons for us to learn from these pictures in the Old Testament; and whether they be types or not, we can learn the lessons that God would have us learn from them.

You notice that the Book of Ruth contains the history of a Jew who went into a far country; in fact, I might say that the first chapter of this book is the fifteenth of Luke over again. We get a Jew backsliding, and through the means of that Jew's backsliding, you will find that a poor Gentile girl is brought out of the Gentile country into the land of blessing. Then this girl marries a rich Jew, Boaz; and there we get a picture of the Lord Jesus Christ marrying the Church. Then after the rich Jew and the poor Gentile are united, you see the blessing turns back to the Jew. And I think that is just what the New Testament teaches of the way in which God is going to deal with the Jew by-and-by. He has backslidden, and the Gentiles are blessed; the Church of God will be united in Christ, and then the Jews will be blessed again.

But what we are going to look at now is the first chapter of this Book of Ruth. You notice that each chapter is perfectly distinct from the other. In this first chapter we get Ruth Deciding; in the second, Ruth Gleaning; in the third, Ruth Resting; and in the fourth, Ruth Rewarded. So that while each chapter is distinct, the whole seems to represent the progress that the Christian makes in the Divine life.

This chapter begins by telling us:

> *"Now it came to pass in the days when the judges ruled, that there was a famine in the land."*

You will find in the history of the Jews, that when God's people had backslidden, famine was one of the punishments sent by Him; therefore the whole nation had gone astray at the time we read of here. (See 2 Kgs. 8:1; Jer. 16:3-13; Ezek. 5:11-17).

> *"And a certain man of Bethlehem-Judah went to sojourn in the country of Moab, he and his wife and his two sons. And the name of the man was Elimelech."*

Elimelech means "God is King." A king is one who has to be obeyed. But as soon as famine comes into the land we find this man is disobedient. As long as everything is prosperous, and right, and well, he is content to serve the king; but as soon as the famine comes he starts for Moab. I dare say there was no famine in Moab, but God had told them to stay in the land of Canaan. They were not to go to Moab at all. Yet as soon as the famine came, the whole family started off to Moab.

I do not know whether it has ever struck you, but human nature is the same the wide world over. You may read about some of the best and brightest characters in the Book of God, and you will find that there was always a tendency to go to Moab—to disobey God. But one thing you will never find—you never find a saint of the living God getting into the wrong place and the wrong position, but he does a great amount of damage.

We cannot be neutral; if we are not a blessing to the world, we shall be a curse. We shall be a blessing if we are in Canaan, and a curse if we go to Egypt. Take the history of Abraham; as soon as the famine came he went straight to Egypt, and you know what happened there. Take the history of Isaac, and it is the same thing—as if he could not trust God in the famine. It does not need much trust when there is plenty; but as soon as the famine came, away they started, and you know what mischief they wrought among the people where they went. And so it is all through the Book.

I know a great many people get downcast about this tendency to evil within them. I used to imagine that I was not a Christian, because I had these tendencies in my heart. But now, if I did not find it so, I could not believe I was a Christian at all, because it would be contrary to the Book. There is a natural tendency in these hearts of ours to go astray, and if it were not for the goodness of God we should go astray all the time.

I was in county Kerry, in Ireland, a little while ago, and I went out into a field along with a gentleman who had a great many sheep. By-and-by we came to a mother sheep, with three of the sweetest little lambs, "Is not that a pretty sight?" I said. "Yes, but I am not going to let her keep them all; I am going to take one of them away." "What will the lamb do?" "I will give it to a goat to bring up." "Did you ever do that before?" "Yes; two years ago that same sheep had three lambs; I gave one of them to a goat to bring up. By-and-by the lamb grew and was able to eat grass; then I took it away from the goat, and put it among the sheep; but that lamb never heard the bleating of a goat but it tried to get after it." What was the reason? It had been brought up on goat's milk, and had thus partaken of the nature of the goat. So it is with the sheep and lambs of Christ. We have been nursed on goat's milk, and when we hear the bleating of the goat we want to go after it. But, thank God, we have a Good Shepherd who knows how to take care of His sheep and lambs.

Well, Naomi went into the land of Moab; and then the worst part of it is, *"she continued there."* Perhaps she went at first to see what kind of place it was, and I've no doubt she found it much better than Canaan, especially in the time of famine.

> *"And Elimelech, Naomi's husband, died; and she was left, and her two sons"* (v. 3).

One evil leads to another. You know there was a law, given by God Himself, that no Hebrew should marry a Moabite: but now she has got into the wrong place—into Moab, and what is the result? Her two sons

> *"Took them wives of the women of Moab; the name of the one was Orpah, and the name of the other Ruth; and they dwelt there about ten years. And Mahlon and Chilion died also, both of them; and the woman was left of her two sons and her husband"* (vv. 4-5).

There is a passage of Scripture that compares Israel at this present day to a widow bereft of her children. So it was with Naomi; she lost her husband and then her two sons.

> *"Then she arose with her daughters-in-law, that she might return from the country of Moab; for she had heard in the country of Moab how that the LORD had visited His people in giving them bread."*

She had tarried in Moab for more than ten years. But now she hears that God has visited His people—and she was certainly poor in this place, because she goes back with nothing. So she says, *"Now I will go back home."*

One sweet thing we always find in the Bible—the true child of the living God never dies in the far country; he goes back to his Father's house. God brings back His people by one way or another.

I know sometimes we see people who make a great profession, so that you would almost think they were angels come from the sky. They make mistakes and never seem to rise again. But if they are truly led by the grace of God they will never die in the far country; they always come back again.

Turn for a minute to Genesis chapter 8 verses 6-8. Here we find that the raven and the dove both went out—both together, perhaps. The dove found no rest for the sole of her foot, but the raven did. It found rest on those putrid carcasses that were floating on the face of the deep. On these the raven could find both rest and food, and why? Because it was a raven. But the dove found neither rest nor food, because it was a dove. They had two different natures. The one came back and the other never did. I fear a good many ravens have crept into the Church. By-and-by the raven and the dove both seem to go; but the one never comes back, while the other does. The true child of God can find no rest in the world. He finds nothing but putrid carcasses, and the dove cannot feed on that. So it was with Naomi; she went away, but, blessed be God, she came back again.

Now we come to one of the saddest scenes that we find in the Bible. Notice these two young widows. The name of the one was Orpah, the name of the other Ruth. The three, Naomi and the two daughters-in-law, start to go to Bethlehem. It says positively that

> *"They went on the way to return unto the land of Judah"* (v. 7).

But in the next two verses we read that Naomi said unto them,

> *"Go, return each to her mother's house;... then she kissed them, and they lifted up their voice and wept."*

I know a great many friends imagine that Naomi did not mean them to go back again; that she was merely testing their faith, to see if they loved her. With all my heart and soul I believe that Naomi meant just what she said; that when she said, *"go back,"* she meant it. When she kissed them, and said "goodbye," she wanted them to turn back again to the dark, sinful land of Moab. Why did she not want to take them to Bethlehem and to the God of her fathers? I will tell you why. She had disobeyed the voice of her God in allowing her sons to marry these Moabites, and she wants to drive them back because she does not like to take evidence of her shame and her sin to Bethlehem, where she came from. I believe, with all my heart and soul, that Orpah's turning back may be laid at the feet of Naomi. I tell you, you and I can either be a curse or a blessing. We can either invite others to the Lord Jesus Christ, or we can drive them from the Lord Jesus Christ. We cannot be neutral; we must be either doing good for the Master or harm. Orpah returned home; but see how she wept with they parted. And we read in the 10th verse that they both said,

> *"Surely we will return with thee unto thy people."*

When they started, they wanted to go—they were determined to go; and the only one to drive Orpah back was one of God' people who had got into Moab. If you are a wanderer from God today, I am sure that in your home, among your friends and among your children, you are a curse and not a blessing! The child of God can be nothing but a curse when he gets into the far country. "Go back!" she said. "No!" they replied. And Naomi used every arguement and every inducement that a woman could use to get them to go back. She prevails on Orpah. She put her arms around her neck, kissed her, said good-bye, and Orpah started off. And now notice Naomi uses another arguement with Ruth. "Why, Ruth, you will be lonely if you come with me. Your sister-in-law has gone back again, will you not go with her?" and Naomi knew, too, **where** she was wishing to send Ruth; listen to the words that came from her lips:

> *"Behold, thy sister-in-law is gone back unto her people* ***and unto her gods****: return thou after thy sister-in-law"* (v. 15, my emphasize).

Driven back to idolatry and sin by an Israelite.

But let us ask ourselves, where are we today? Are we in Moab or in Canaan? Are we in the far country or at home? I tell you, as sure as we are in Moab, we shall be the means of driving many an Orpah back to her gods and to sin. But Ruth had made up her mind. It was not Naomi who induced her to go. I do not believe that beautiful jewel will ever deck the crown of Naomi. She did all she could to drive her back; but the grace of God had touched the heart of Ruth. She is not going to return; she is going to Bethlehem. How Naomi must have **entreated** her to go back! Because we read that Ruth said to Naomi,

> *"Entreat me not to leave thee, or to return from following after thee; for whither thou goest I will go, and where thou lodgest I will lodge"* (v. 16).

What a sweet word! Not "where thou **dwellest**," but "where thou **lodgest**." The Church of God is never anything else but a lodger down here, even in the midst of the fields of Boaz.

> *"Thy people shall be my people, and thy God my God. Where thou diest, I will die, and there will I be buried; the Lord do so to me, and more also, if aught but death part thee and me. When she saw that she was steadfastly minded to go with her, then she left speaking unto her. So they two went until they came to Bethlehem. And it came to pass, when they were come to Bethlehem, that all the city was moved about them, and they said, 'Is that Naomi?'"* (vv. 16-19).

As if they had said "Naomi, who is this you have brought into our country? Is this the Naomi who went away with her husband and two sons, come back with a poor Gentile girl?" She said, *"Do not call me Naomi, that used to be my name, but call me Marah."* What for? Marah means "bitterness," while Naomi means "pleasant." *"Because the Almighty hath dealt very bitterly with me."* She blames the Almighty for what had happened to her. The only part the Almighty had in it was, in grace, bringing her back again. She had disobeyed, and had no one to blame but herself, yet she blames the Almighty! There is many a child of God whose name is Naomi, but they have lost that sweet name. It is Marah now, because they have gone into a far country. Thank God, when we do get into Moab we lose our name, because we lose our joy. Moab is the land of bitterness to the child of God, and thank God it is so. If it were not so, perhaps, we should like to die and be buried there.

Notice what she says. *"I went out."* That was quite true. It was **"I"** that went out. *"And the Lord hath brought me home again."* She does not say the Lord took her away and she came back again, but *"**I** went out and **the Lord** hath brought me home."* It is the old story of the poor sheep that went away. The sheep went astray but the shepherd brought it back again.

Is there not something very sweet about that little word *"Home"*? he has brought me **home** again! It is one of the sweetest words, I think, in this blessed Book, next to Jesus. "Home, sweet Home!" I was crossing the Atlantic some time ago with my friend, Mr. Moody, and on board the same ship there was a band of Italian tunes and sing Italian airs, but I could not make out their words. One night I said to Mr. Moody, "It would be so nice if they would play 'Home, sweet Home.'" Mr. Moody spoke about it to a gentleman who could speak Italian, and he went and asked if they would play "Home, sweet Home." The man said, "We could not play that." "Why?" "Well, we do not know the meaning of it; we have not got such a word as 'home' in our language." Some people talk about the sweet, beautiful Italian tongue; I would rather have the good, old Saxon that has got the word *"home"* than any language in the world that has not got that sweet word. This is the language of the Bible. The world has not got such a word: it is the Christian who has got the word *"home."*

"The Lord hath brought me home again empty" (v. 21).

If we go away, the Lord will bring us back again by one means or another. Shortly after I was converted I used to go and speak for the Lord at a place in Lancashire. There I got acquainted with a Wesleyan and his wife. He and I became good friends; he seemed a dear Christian. Soon after that I went away to Ireland. When I was returning again, I wrote to him to say I was coming; I expected to see him at the station. When I arrived he was not there. I went and called upon him—I was sure he would be glad to see me. But when a person gets away from Christ, he never likes to see a Christian. Of course he shook hands with me, but it was in such a cold way, I knew something was wrong. I found out what it was; he had got rich. Now, do not misunderstand me. It is no sin to be rich if God makes you rich, or if you use the riches for His glory. The sin is when you have your heart set on riches.

My friend had bought a lot of land and had got rich without work. Of course he could not go to worship with the poor Methodist fishermen then. He became a backslider, and cared for nothing but making money, Money, MONEY; as if there was nothing good in the world but money. I found that his wife had gone back with him, and the daughter had gone with the father and mother. I wondered how it was with John, his son, who was a particular friend of mine. I went and met the father's boat as it came into the harbour. "Well, John, how is it with you?" "Thank God," he said, "it is all right with me; but there are my poor father and mother and sister. I could lay down my life to see them brought back again to the feet of Christ!"

On the Sunday night after, this young man stood up in the meeting and gave his experience. He made use of these remarkable words again, "I could lay down my life to see them brought back again to the feet of Christ!" Next morning he kissed his wife and little child, and with some other friends started on board his father's boat to go to sea. He was doing something, when the boat gave a lurch, and he was thrown into the water. He was one of the best and strongest swimmers, but he had his heavy sailor's jacket on. Before they had time to tack and come around they saw his uplifted hands, they heard him cry out something about the Precious Blood of Christ, and he sank to rise no more, till the sea shall give up its dead.

By-and-by the old father said to his little boy Richard, "Run down and see if there are any tidings of the boat." The little fellow came back an hour afterwards, his face pale, and tears running down his cheeks. "Oh, father, father!" he sobbed. "What is the matter? Have they lost their nets in the fog?" "Oh, father, it is worse than that. They have lost our John! Our John is not in the boat! He is fallen overboard and he is drowned!" The poor old man burst into tears. He called for his wife and said, "Get down on thy knees, lass; God has ta'en our John from us. It is all our fault; we were heaping up that money for him. God has ta'en our John, and the money is of no use. Let us ask God to pardon us." So they asked God's forgiveness, and I saw that man afterwards preaching the glorious gospel of the Lord Jesus Christ. But oh, at what a cost!

Naomi is brought back; but think of the cost:

> *"The Lord hath testified against me, and the Almighty hath afflicted me"* (v. 21).

The light of her eyes, the darling of her heart—taken from her! Yea, brother, sister, God will bring you back. And if I am speaking to one who has gone into Moab, will you not come back today, and now? Come and confess your sins to the Lord Jesus Christ and He will pardon you. Come and make a clean breast of it; tell Him everything. Come back to Canaan at *"the beginning of the barley harvest"* as Naomi did, and God will bless and help you.

May God incline our hearts to come back to His feet at once; then we will be able to work more successfully than ever before, but we must be at the feet of the Lord Jesus Christ, where God would have us be.

Chapter 2
Ruth Gleaning

This chapter begins by telling us about the kinsman, of the name of Boaz, who was *"a mighty man of wealth."* I think that this expression, *"a mighty man of wealth,"* is not found in the Scriptures anywhere except here; and you know that Boaz was a picture of the Lord Jesus Christ, who became our kinsman. We do not propose to speak so much about the kinsman here, because we hope to mention him again. But it is well for us to know that we have got a kinsman who is *"a mighty man of wealth."* There is no necessity why God's people should be poor; I do not mean poor in purse, because sometimes it is a blessed privilege for God's people to be poor in that respect.

But I am sure none need be poor in spiritual things, because everything our *"mighty man of wealth"* possesses is given to us. You know that wonderful Scripture, *"Though He was rich, yet for your sakes He became poor, that ye through His poverty might be rich"* (2 Cor. 8:9). And a man who has not got a shilling in the world, if he is a Christian, is far richer than the richest millionaire who is not a Christian, because he possesses Christ, and all that the *"mighty man of wealth"* owns belongs to him.

Now, do you not see that Ruth was a woman who had a great deal of faith; she believed the word of God. She said to Naomi,

> *"Let me now go to the field and glean ears of corn after him in whose sight I shall find grace"* (v. 2).

How did she know that she had got any right to glean in the fields? Because God, under whose wings she had come to trust, had told His people because they entered the land, that this was to be the privilege of the poor and the stranger. She takes the place of the stranger; she goes to glean in the fields of Boaz.

I do not know whether you have ever noticed that in the

Scriptures there is a great deal said about gleaning, and about the way in which we are to treat the gleaners. Turn to Deuteronomy 24:19-21:

> *"When thou cuttest down thine harvest in thy field, and hast forgot a sheaf in the field thou shalt not go again to fetch it: it shall be for the stranger, for the fatherless, and for the widow; that the* Lord *thy God may bless thee in all the work of thine hands. When thou beatest thine olive-tree, thou shalt not go over the boughs again; it shall be for the stranger, for the fatherless, and for the widow. When thou gatherest the grapes of thy vineyard, thou shalt not glean it afterward: it shall be for the stranger, for the fatherless, and for the widow."*

If we were to put a mark to every passage in this book of Deuteronomy where God speaks about the stranger, the father-less and the widow, and find out how God wants us to treat them, I am sure there would not be so many Christians pining for work as there are—who cannot find anything to do for God. It is one of the blessed principles laid down in the Old Testament and taught in the New, that we should be kind to the stranger, the fatherless and the widow. And the claim they have upon us is their very helplessness.

In this beautiful passage in Deuteronomy about gleaning, it speaks of the harvest, of the olive, and of the grape. You say, "Well, I am not a farmer, I know nothing of harvest. Olives do not grow in this cold country. And it is only a few people in this land who can grow grapes. What is the meaning of this?" I will tell you what it means, because when God tells us to deal in this way with the stranger, and the fatherless, and the widow, He means us to do it. You know what the harvest means. It was the ingathering of the corn, and you know what that was for—to be made into bread. And you know what bread was for—to give strength; then the olive was a symbol of fruitfulness, and the grape typified joy. So then the three things God teaches us here to do, are to give strength and peace and joy to the stranger, the fatherless, and the widow. You will find Ruths everywhere, and

God wants us to give them the corn, to give them the olive, and to give them the vine.

How can we do this? Turn to Proverbs 12:25, and let us see how we can do it for the Master. (I am going to take the very lowest thing it is possible for a child of God to do. I am not going to speak of those who can give their hundreds and thousands of dollars and be none the poorer; but let the very poorest of us see if we cannot be the means of bringing strength and peace and joy to those who need it.) *"Heaviness in the heart of man maketh it stoop."* We all know that is true. What is going to make it glad? A fifty-dollar note? No! A hundred-dollar note? No! *"But a good word maketh it glad."*

It is not only the wealth or the riches that God speaks about. Here it is a kind, loving word, *"a good word,"* that makes the heart glad. You know this world is full of heavy hearts and drooping souls. And I am very sorry to say that too many of us Christians seem to think that good words cost a small fortune apiece, from the way we give them to those who need them. God wants us to speak kind words, good words.

Did you ever consider, did you ever compare **the words** of the Lord Jesus Christ, and His **works**, His miracles? Why, the Lord Jesus accomplished more by His words than by His miracles. I do not know how many people He healed; I do not know how many people He raised from the dead. It may have been fifty, or five thousand, or fifty thousand; but there have been millions and millions brought to glory, and millions on millions cheered down here by the loving **words** of the Lord Jesus Christ. And He wants us to be imitators of Him. When He was here He had no long purse, but He had a kind word for everybody except the self-satisfied, the self-righteous, the Scribes and the Pharisees. He had a loving word of sympathy for every class. We, too, can give these and be none the poorer for it.

Turn to Isaiah 1:4: *"The Lord God hath given me the tongue of the learned, that I should know how to speak a word in season to him that is weary."* Perhaps you say, "Oh, I would like to have the tongue of the learned to show people how clever I am!" The Lord Jesus had *"the tongue of the learned"* for one purpose, and that was to know how to speak a word in season to him that was weary. Here again it is the word; it is not the power or the miracle (Read: Colossians 3:17). It was only recently that this struck me with such force; I never noticed it before. *"Whatsoever ye do in word or deed, do all in the name of the Lord Jesus, giving thanks to God and the Father by Him."* Has it ever occurred to you that is a very strange way of putting it, *"Whatsoever ye do* ***in word*** *or* ***deed****"*? We may be disposed to think it ought to have been, "Whatsoever ye **say in word** or do in need." But it is not so: *"Whatsoever ye* ***do in word*** *or deed."* As if God said: "Every word you speak for Me is a good work." And what we want is to have *"the tongue of the learned,"* to know how to speak a word to those that are weary.

If we want to be happy, if we want to be joyful and glad, let us try to make others glad. Let us try to give them strength, and peace, and joy. The most miserable man today is the man who lives for self; the happiest man is the one who forgets self, and lives for others. There is no true happiness when we are thinking of self, and living for self; it is only when self is denied, the cross carried, and we are working and speaking for others, that we are happy indeed. What a sweet thing it is to know that God has told us, *"Whatsoever ye* ***do in word****."* Up yonder He is keeping a record of it.

A person says, "Don't I wish sometimes that I had got the purse of Baron Rothschild, or the purse of Baron Burdett-Coutts." Beloved friend, if God had wanted you to have the purse of Baron Rothschild, He would have given it to you. You have got a tongue, and, if you have got Christ in your heart, use that tongue for the Master, to cheer the widow, to comfort the fatherless, and to lighten the heart of the afflicted. That is what God wants us to do. And we shall be as happy as the day is long, if we obey our loving God.

I remember at one time I got down-hearted, cloudy, and dark. It was a miserable day; at least, I was miserable. I think Christians ought not to be miserable, no matter what kind of days there are. But I was down-hearted that day. It was Christmas Eve, and there was a thick fog all over Manchester, where I was, and the miserable, sleety rain was coming down. I looked at my watch, and it was about eight o'clock. Four miles away there was a little cottage, with a bright fire and a nice cup of tea ready for me. I thought to myself, "I will get right home, and make myself comfortable."

But at that moment I thought about a little child two miles away. There were no busses and no cars; I should have to trudge all the way, and it was Christmas Eve. I began to think, "Well now, little girls will expect presents tomorrow; I wonder if anybody has taken anything to this little child. It will be eleven o'clock before I get home if I go, and what will my wife say to my coming home so late? And I shall have to walk through the rain, and the slush, and the mud, and the fog." Something whispered, "I would not do it, if I were you." But then another thought came: "Suppose that child were your little Mamie, and there was no one to give her anything."

I went into a toy-shop, bought a doll for a few coppers, and started off through the cold and wet.

By-and-by I came to a cellar, where this child lived with her mother and little brother. I knocked at the door and the voice said, "Come in." I put my thumb on the latch and went inside. There was a miserable little bit of fire, and no candle. By the light of the fire I saw the little boy sitting on one side, and lying on the bed there was the little girl, about nine years old. She was suffering from a terrible disease, and amputation of a limb had become necessary. She said to me, "I am so glad that you have come; nobody has been able to see us, and my mother has gone out to see if she could get anything to do, and get some money to buy Christmas dinner with." I said, "I have come to give you a doll," and gave it to her. The little thing looked at it; then she put her hand into the bed, and took out some old rags. She said, "I have been trying to make a doll myself; oh, how nice to have a real one."

She took the doll and kissed it. In a moment the darkness had gone from my spirit; the cold chilly feeling had disappeared, and I was as happy as ever I could be, I would not have missed taking that doll, that only cost a few pennies, for a ten dollar note. How glad it had made me! And the next day the happiness I had in seeing my own little girl was ten times more, because I knew another little girl was made happy too. Everywhere you go you will find gleaners—poor Ruths, who need something; and God tells you to give them strength, and peace, and joy.

Now in verse four of this chapter it says:

> *"And, behold, Boaz came from Bethlehem, and said unto the reapers, 'The LORD be with you;' And they answered him, 'The LORD bless thee.'"*

You never read any of a strike among Boaz' workmen; he treated them too kindly for that. Just fancy the master coming along, and the first words he says are, *"The LORD be with you;"* and they stand up and say, *"The LORD bless thee."* I do not know whether these servants quarrelled amongst themselves in the morning. No doubt they had little quarrels, and some of them did not always speak kindly to one another. But when the master came, he spoke kindly to them. And we can always go to our Master for a kind, loving word.

Boaz asks, "Whose damsel is this?" And the reapers reply, "That is Ruth, the Moabitess. She has come with Naomi from Moab. She is very poor. Naomi has got nothing for her, so she has come to glean." So Boaz turns to her, and says (v. 8):

> *"Hearest thou not, my daughter? Go not to glean in another field, neither go from hence, but abide here fast by my maidens."*

What wonderful significance there is in the first words he spoke to her, *"Go not to glean in another field."* Why? "Because I am a mighty man of wealth. All the fields around belong to me; I have got plenty to satisfy you." Do you remember what the Lord Jesus tells His people? *"Love not the world"*—go not to glean in another field. You know what gleaning means—getting something to satisfy yourself with. So the Lord said, "Do not go and look for anything to satisfy you outside of My fields." I will tell you why there is so much sorrow in the Church of God, so many sad hearts amongst God's people, so much coldness and deadness. It is because the people of God have gone to glean in another field besides that of the Master. It is because we do not think He has got enough to satisfy us. We have not obeyed the Master. We have got a craving for something else than His blessed Word. What is the result? Sorrow, sadness, and darkness have come over our souls.

I sometimes think this is what we read of in Numbers 11:4. *"The mixed multitude that was amongst them fell a lusting, and the children of Israel also wept again."* The first time they wept after they had crossed the Red Sea was because they had got into bad company—people who had not been sheltered by the blood of the paschal Lamb. They became mixed, and the result was weeping and sorrow. We sometimes imagine that the Master makes mistakes, and that we should not be happy if we obey Him. But God wants us to be happy; He wants us to be true and faithful, and we cannot be happy unless we are.

In Nehemiah 13:23, we read: *"In those days also I saw Jews that had married wives of Ashdod, of Ammon, and of Moab."* They, so to speak, had gone into other fields to seek for something that they thought God would not give them. *"And their children spake half in the speech of Ashdod, and could not speak in the Jews' language, but according to the language of each people."* I think this is a picture of the Church at the present day. Take nine professing Christians out of ten, and you will find you cannot tell to whom they belong; for the first five minutes you will think that they belong to Christ; then in the next five they seem to belong to the world. They do not speak either language correctly. It is Christianity on Sundays, and the world on week days.

God requires that we should come right out, and be separate. *"Be ye separate." "Be ye holy, as I am holy."* Do not let us try to speak the language of Ashdod one day, and the language of the Hebrew the next. Let us be decided for Christ or for the world. Let us get the question settled. If we are Christians, let us be out and out for Christ. If we are not, do not let us make a false profession; taking the place of Christians before men, when we are not so before God. **Let us be what we are.**

The Spring is coming on, and by-and-by you will go into the fields. There is a lark there—and how sweetly it sings! Did you ever hear a lark sing in its nest? No. Now stand and listen. By-and-by the lark begins to rise, and it begins to sing. As the little bird gets higher, it sings the louder, higher still and louder still; and it sings the loudest when it gets so high that you cannot see it at all. The lark sings its very sweetest then. And you can always tell when it is coming down. The moment it begins to come down, it begins to lose its song. The nearer it gets to the earth the less it sings, until at last it sinks into its nest, and the song ceases altogether. Is not that the way with Christians? We go and build a pretty little nest, and we do not sing. But as soon as we begin to rise we sing. The higher we get the sweeter we sing – higher still and sweeter still. And when we sing the loudest and the sweetest is when we get so high in Christ that the world cannot see us for our Master.

Oh, my brother, my sister, listen to this advice: *"Go not to glean in another field."* There is nought but hay and stubble there. But there are wheat, and barley, and corn for you in the Master's fields. The Master tells you to tarry and glean. He will give you plenty.

The next advice that Boaz gives to Ruth is this:

> *"'Let thine eyes be on the field that they do reap, and go then after them: have I not charged the young men that they shall not touch thee? And when thou art athirst, go unto the vessels, and drink of that which the young men have drawn.' Then she fell on her face, and bowed herself to the ground and said unto him, 'Why have I found grace in thine eyes, that thou shouldst take knowledge of me, seeing I am a stranger?' And Boaz answered and said unto her, 'It hath fully been showed to me, all that thou hast done unto they mother-in-law since the death of thine husband; and how thou hast left thy father and thy mother, and the land of thy nativity, and art come unto a people which thou knewest not heretofore"* (vv. 9-11).

We see here that all the love of Ruth to Naomi was known to Boaz.

Perhaps you are a worker for the Lord; you have been trying to do something for Him who redeemed you. At times you get fearfully discouraged. You are working away, perhaps, in some little dark street; the rain or snow is coming down; perhaps your boots are not water-proof, and you have not got a very good cloak to put on. But you start off on Sunday afternoon, and when you get there you find five or six people gathered. You tell them the truth, but they seem perfectly indifferent, and the word does not appear to have any effect. You go there Sunday after Sunday. Perhaps you go week after week and visit the sick and the poor, but nobody comes and pats you on the back and says you are doing a good work. Nobody puts a nice little notice in the paper about your work. And you get discouraged because nobody takes any notice. Nobody took any notice of Ruth, but Boaz said, "I know all about it." And I would rather that the Lord took knowledge of my work than anybody else. He will not forget those dreary days when you walked down to teach those people about His beloved Son. Take courage, my brother, my sister. You may have to go through the rain and the mud; but there never was an angel in heaven yet who had the privilege of catching a cough or a cold for Jesus. They never did, and they never can. *"It hath fully been showed to me all that thou hast done for thy mother-in-law since the death of thine husband."* He knew everything.

Then look what he says:

> *"'The LORD recompense thy work, and a full reward be given thee of the LORD God of Israel, under whose wings thou art come to trust.' Then she said, 'Let me find favour in thy sight, my lord; for that thou hast comforted me and for that thou hast spoken friendly unto thine handmaid"* (vv. 12-13).

You will notice in the margin it is *"spoken* ***to the heart*** *of thine handmaid."* That is what the Lord always speaks to. I never find the Lord speaking much to people's brains, or their intellects.

He always speaks right to the one place, and that is the heart. And that is where every child of God ought to aim at. You may put out a man's eye, and it will only blind him; but you cannot put a knife into a man's heart without killing him. So, if the word of God gets into a man's heart, he will be killed to self, and made alive to God.

Then Boaz says:

> *"At meal time come thou hither, and eat of the bread and dip thy morsel in the vinegar. And she sat beside the reapers"* (v. 14).

She always did what he told her, and that was why she got so many blessings. She did not say, "I am too poor," or "I have not got the right kind of costume." Whatever Boaz told her to do she did; and what was the result? She was blessed. So with us; we should not be always telling the Lord we are so humble we do not like to obey Him. We ought to do what He tells us, whatever it is. The Lord never gives us a command, but He wants us to obey it. He will give us strength for obedience.

"At meal time come thou hither." The Lord does not want His people to be always working; He wants them to have some food as well. We all like meal times, especially when we are hungry. It is right for us to have proper meal times. I wonder what we would think of a house where they kept us six days without any food, and the seventh day they piled up all kinds of dainties and we ate so much we did not know what to do! Six days' starving and one day's feeding! Yet that is the way many Christians do. They go and eat once a week as if they could take enough at one meal to last them for a whole week. You cannot do it. Christ taught His disciples to pray, *"Give us today our daily bread."* I cannot eat today what is going to do for tomorrow. And there would not be so many weak, powerless Christians if they would have proper meal times, and sit daily at the Master's feet. More and more my daily prayer is, "Lord, give me my daily bread, my daily strength, and my daily work." I do not want Him to give me tomorrow's strength or tomorrow's work, but today's strength and today's work. And He will give it.

"She came and sat down beside the reapers, and he reached her parched corn." He fed her. And the Lord will feed us if we will just obey Him. He will take care that we get enough. *"And she did eat, and was sufficed, and left."* But you say, was not that a waste of time? Why was she not gleaning all this while? She just did what Boaz told her. And now he takes the servants aside and he says: *"Let fall also some of the handful of purpose for her, and leave them, that she may glean them."* If it had not been for the master, she would never have got anything but single ears of barley. But as soon as she obeyed him, he told the servants to let fall *"handfuls of purpose"* for her, *"and reproach her not."* Do not tell her she is getting too much; that her pile is accumulating too fast. Ruth was a woman of faith. She did not say, "It is too much," but took up handful after handful, until even came. We sometimes think, "All these promises of God for us! They are too many." But if God has chosen to give them, surely it is as little as we can do to pick them up. Ruth got more by sitting that half hour at the master's feet, then she had got altogether before. It was grace that did it. And when we get up yonder, and look back on the past, we will see how many *"handfuls of purpose"* have been dropped for us.

You remember that day you went out with a sad heart. You had not got very far before you met that friend "by accident" of course who spoke so lovingly to you, and cheered you on your way. Another day you met a friend; "it was so fortunate," you thought; it was such a happy accident you turned down that street. No, no; your friend came with a handful of blessing to drop *"of purpose."* God sent the blessing. There was no such thing as chance or accident about it. All the way along we find our path way strewn with handfuls *"of purpose"* for us.

"So she gleaned in the field until even." She did not work for an hour and then run away; she kept at it hour after hour, all the day long, until even came. Then just look at what she had gleaned. More than she could carry away! Now, there is one thing the Bible is silent about, and that is what kind of a woman Ruth was. It does not tell us the colour of her eyes, or the colour of her hair, or anything of that sort. If we were writing about her, we would say she had such and such a complexion, or that

her hair was such and such a colour. That is not the way God does. But He does tell us, or leaves us to infer, that she was a woman who had a great deal of faith, and a great deal of common sense.

You know it is one thing to have grace, and another thing to have common sense. But she had both. She had got more than she wanted, and *"she beat out that she had gleaned; and it was about an ephah of barley."* And she carried away—the straw? No, she did not; but that is what we do sometimes. We attend a meeting, and when we go away we leave the corn behind, and carry away the straw only. "Dear me! Never heard any thing like that before." "Do you agree with all that he said?" "He said this or he said that, or he said the other: did you know what it all meant?" That is carrying away the straw instead of the wheat. The wheat cannot grow without straw, and many sermons have more straw than wheat in them. Beat it out. Leave the straw and carry home the wheat. I never heard anybody in my life who spoke about the Master, who did not give me some wheat to carry away. Let us glean until even, then beat it out and carry home the wheat or the barley.

> *"And her mother-in-law said unto her, 'Where hast thou gleaned today? And where wroughtest thou? Blessed be he that did take knowledge of thee.' And she showed her mother-in-law with whom she had wrought, and said, 'The man's name with whom I wrought today is Boaz.' And Naomi said unto her, 'The man is near of kin unto us, one of our next kinsmen.' And Ruth the Moabitess said, 'He said unto me also, "Thou shalt keep fast by my young men, until they have ended all my harvest."' And Naomi said unto Ruth her daughter-in-law, 'It is good, my daughter, that thou go out with his maidens, that they meet thee not in any other field.' So she kept fast by the maidens of Boaz to glean until the end of the barley harvest and of wheat harvest; and dwelt with her mother-in-law"* (v. 19-23).

We will next consider "Ruth Resting," not "gleaning." May the Lord help us to go and try if we cannot find some poor Ruth for whom we may drop some *"handfuls of purpose"* gathered in the Master's name, and for the Saviour's sake.

Chapter 3
Ruth Resting

I suppose you have noticed that the second chapter concludes with the end of the harvest, both of barley and of wheat. The wheat harvest came after the barley harvest. And we read: *"She* [Ruth] *kept fast by the maidens of Boaz to glean unto the end of barley harvest and of wheat harvest, and dwelt with her mother-in-law."* In this chapter we do not read anything about the harvest for her now. What is to become of Ruth and Naomi?

It is a blessed thing to find out that the Scriptures teach us we are not dependent on means. We are dependent on the Master, and not on means. We sometimes hear people mourning because they cannot go to the "means of grace." Sometimes when we cannot get to the so-called means of grace is the time when we are nearest to grace itself, because we are forced to go to the Master, who is *"full of grace and truth."* Grace is far better than the means of grace. The Lord Jesus Christ will take care that His people shall not want anything if they are obedient.

This chapter begins with a wonderful question:

> *"My daughter, shall I not seek rest for thee, that it may be well with thee?"*

There is a wonderful difference between this language and that used by Naomi in the 9th verse of the first chapter. There she says to Ruth and Orpah: *"The LORD grant you* ***that ye may find rest****, each of you in the house of her husband."* When Naomi was in Moab, she did not appear to manifest the same tender care for them; but now she is at Bethlehem, and has eaten of the grain that came from the fields of Boaz, see how different is her language. *"****Shall I seek rest*** *for thee?"* When we are in the far country, and out of communion with the Lord, we do not care where sinners go to; but when our hearts are right, we will use the language of Naomi. We will not mind if we have to travel ten miles to take a message from the Master to some poor, lost, guilty sinner. In one case we may indeed express the desire: *"The Lord grant you that you may find rest,"* but in the other it is: *"Shall I not seek rest for thee?"*

In the second verse Naomi tells Ruth something that perhaps she did not know; and it is something that seems to be forgotten by the Church of God in the present day.

> *"Is not Boaz of our kindred with whose maidens thou wast? Behold, he winnoweth barley tonight in the threshing floor."*

There had been some one to plough the land, and some one to sow the seed, and some one to reap the harvest; and the history does not tell us the names of these servants. But when it comes to the winnowing, it tells us that Boaz himself is going to do it. Sometimes I come across workers who are discouraged because they do not see results. I am a worker, and I want to encourage any one who is working for the Lord Jesus Christ. Do not get discouraged because you see some one else who is a great deal more successful in winning souls than you are.

I once lived next door to a farmer, and I used to see him when he went out to sow his fields. I said to him one day: "Why do you do that yourself?" "Because," he said, "I have not got a servant whom I can trust to sow. I had one once whom I could trust, but he has left me. I must have one to sow the seed, in whom I can put confidence." I have seen that very farmer go and hire the first Irish labourer that come along, to put in the sickle to reap. Who did the most important work? Not the man who reaped, but the man who sowed. So you, perhaps, who are toiling and labouring for the Lord Jesus Christ, you never see a soul won to the Saviour. Thank God for the great honour He is conferring upon you in making you a sower, even if He makes somebody else the reaper. *"One soweth and another reapeth,"* but, *"neither is he that planteth anything, neither he that watereth, but God that giveth the increase"* (John 4:37; 1 Cor. 3:7). Sow the seed beside all waters, and by-and-by, both sower and reaper shall rejoice together. When the Master winnoweth the barley, we will all get the praise that is due to us. Perhaps some poor old woman who has never been off her bed for ten years, will get more praise than one who seemed to win thousands of souls to Christ. The Master will give every one the right reward.

"Behold, he winnoweth barley tonight in the threshing floor." I think there is something very instructive about this. *"He winnoweth barley."* Every man's work is going to be tried and tested. You know what the winnowing was for – to separate the barley or the wheat from the chaff. The wind blew all the chaff away, and there was nothing left but pure grain. Perhaps, when some of us come to have our work tried, a good deal will be blown away; but, thank God, the grain will remain. The chaff will be blown away, for we shall not want it then.

Let us now turn to a few passages of Scripture in connection with winnowing. Paul says: *"If any man build upon this foundation, gold, silver, precious stones, wood, hay, stubble, every man's work shall be made manifest; for the day shall declare it, because it shall be revealed by fire; and the fire shall try every man's work of what sort it is. If any man's work abide, which he hath built thereupon, he shall receive a reward. If any man's work shall be burned, he shall suffer loss; but he himself shall be saved, yet so as by fire"* (1 Cor. 3:10-15). Not everybody in this world is a builder; but all the members of the true Church of Christ are builders. God Himself has laid the foundation-stone, which is Jesus Christ, and we are building upon it. Here we see that each man's work shall be made manifest and tried. If a man's work abide, he shall receive a reward; for *"every man shall receive his own reward according to his own labour"* (v. 8), but if any man's work shall be burned [does not stand the test], he shall suffer loss [lose the reward]. Therefore let each one take heed to his work, how he builds. Let us take care that our work is done in God's way, and for His glory, and not in man's way, or for the glory of self.

Paul says that we can build gold, silver, precious stones, or we can build wood, hay, stubble. I do not think it is a difficult thing for us to tell which is the gold, silver, precious stones, or which is the wood, hay, stubble. Everything that is done for the glory of self, my work is going to be burnt up as wood, hay, stubble; I do not care what the result may be. If I have preached for the glory of self, my work is going to be burnt up as wood, hay, stubble. What is the gold, silver and precious stones? Everything that is done for the Lord Jesus Christ. You may give a cup of cold water to a beggar in the name of the Lord Jesus, because he belongs to Christ, and you will have your reward. The barley must be winnowed. The work must be tried. Who is going to try it? Not the servants; not the angels. The Lord Jesus Christ will try the work Himself, and all that is wood, hay, stubble, will be burnt up.

Now turn to Revelation 2:10: *"Be thou faithful unto death, and I will give thee a crown of life."* Here we have a blessed truth brought out. A great many people understand this to mean that if we are faithful to God, after we are converted, until we die, He will give us everlasting life—that eternal life depends on our faithfulness. That is not taught here. It is not taught by any Scripture that I can find from Genesis to Revelation. It is, *"Be thou faithful unto death, and I will give thee a* ***crown****."* Did God ever give eternal life to any one because he was faithful? If God did that, hell would be peopled and heaven would be empty. The great fact that we are all sinners shows that we have not been faithful; and it is only on the ground of grace that we can receive eternal life. We receive it as a gift, not as a reward. But when I am saved, and have got eternal life, God says, *"Be thou faithful unto death, and I will reward you."* Just as it is with scholars at school, when vacation time comes. Those who have studied hard, and have become perfect in their lessons, or have got so many marks, receive a prize, which they take home, and show to their mother and father. God is going to give us rewards by-and-by if we are faithful. We do not get **life**, but a **crown** of life, for our faithfulness to Him. The work will be tried and the servant rewarded, because of his work.

There is another passage—1 Corinthians 9:24-27—over which a great many people stumble, but it is in connection with the same subject. Many people understand this to mean that Paul, after all he had suffered, and after all his labours for the Lord Jesus Christ, might be damned. But what does it mean? If anybody will read the context, they will find that it is very simple. What does Paul say? We are all running a race. Who is running? Not unsaved men, but Christians. What are we running for? A prize. But eternal life is not a prize; it is a free gift. What is the prize? A crown. *"So run ye that ye may obtain"* a crown of life, an incorruptible crown. *"I have therefore so run,"* says Paul, *"lest that by any means when I have preached to others, I myself should be a castaway."* The Greek word that is translated here "castaway" means "disapproved"; lest when the Master comes, I shall be disapproved, and lose my crown.

Beloved friends, let us keep our body under; let us be temperate in all things. *"Let us lay aside every weight, and the sin which doth so easily beset us, and let us run with patience the race that is set before us, looking unto Jesus"* (Heb. 12:2-3); not to get eternal life, but to get this blessed crown that our Lord has so graciously promised to us. There will be some in that day who will have so much wheat, that they will have a grand crown. Others, perhaps, will have so much chaff, that they will be disapproved. Each will be rewarded according to his faithfulness. We might quote other passages if needed; but let us go on to the third verse of this chapter, and see the advice of Naomi.

> *"Wash thyself, therefore, and anoint thee, and put thy raiment upon thee, and get thee down to the floor; but make not thyself known unto the man until he shall have done eating and drinking."*

She was going to take her place at the feet of Boaz; and there was as much faith required to do that as to go and glean in the fields. It was her right place to take at the feet of her kinsman.

Notice the three things that are necessary before she could take her place at the feet of Boaz. *"Wash thyself; anoint thee; put thy raiment upon thee."* I need hardly tell you what all this means. Washing means purity. So, if we should lie at the Saviour's feet, we have got to be pure. Anointing signified sanctification; and covering, righteousness. Is there not a grand and glorious truth told us here? Are not these things just what Jesus Himself is to us when we accept Him? The moment we believe we are, as to our standing, pure, as He is pure, He is unto us sanctification and righteousness. And the very things He gives to us are the very things that make us fit to go into His presence. We have not space to refer to it here, but if, at your leisure, you will read the 16th chapter of Ezekiel, you will find these three things brought out in connection with Israel. But if we would sit at the feet of Jesus, and have fellowship with Him, we must be holy in practice, separated from evil, and habitually walking in God's righteous ways; for *"God is light"* and *"if we say that we have fellowship with Him, and walk in darkness, we lie, and do not the truth"* (1 John 1:5-6).

What a grand thing it is to be in the world, as we are, and to have communion with Christ and with God – every action pure and sanctified! I had some plants in my garden, and people used to come and admire those plants. After they had gone out of the garden they would say, "What a sweet flavour there is about me." Do you know where they got it? There was one plant sent to me and I hardly thought it worth putting in the garden at all. I thought it had been spoiled. But I had it put there and it bloomed and blossomed. The flower was not a very pretty one; it had not much show about it. But you could not touch the plant without receiving a sweet savour from it, and the more you pressed it the sweeter was the savour it gave out. There are some Christians just like that flower. You go to their home and you see nothing particular there, no show, no grandeur, perhaps it is the home of some poor Christian woman. You go away, and all the day there is such a sweetness clinging about you, and you wonder where it came from. It is from that lovely plant. The world, perhaps, did not admire her much. She never stood on a platform and preached. She never displayed any eloquence or beauty of language. But you have touched her, and you have carried away some of the sweetness that was there.

There are some other Christians who remind me of what happened when I was a boy. I used to visit a friend, and she would say to me, "Wouldn't you like to take some roses home for your mother?" "No," I said, "I would rather take some nettles." My mother used to take the nettles and boil them, in order to make a kind of spring drink. So I said I would take some nettles. We went to gather them, and got pretty well stung. As we were going home in the train, an old lady came in, and said, "Oh dear me, they are nettles!" So it is with some Christians; they might carry roses if they would, but it seems as if they had got a bag of nettles, and everybody that touches them is stung. It is an awful thing to have a bad tongue, but some of us seem to be content with that; we sting everybody. My friends, it is as cheap to carry roses as nettles. Let us leave the nettles, and carry the roses; let us be sweet Christians, and not stinging ones.

> *"'And it shall be, when he lieth down, that thou shalt mark the place where he shall lie; and thou shalt go in and uncover his feet, and lay thee down; and he will tell thee what thou shalt do.' And she said unto her, 'All that thou sayest unto me I will do'"* (vv. 4-5).

I wish we had more Ruths who just do what they are told. And what a blessed thing for her to get rest. There are two rests spoken of in Matthew 11:28-29. *"Come unto Me and I will give you rest."* That is for the sinner. *"Take My yoke upon you, and learn of Me, for I am meek and lowly in heart, and ye shall find rest for your souls."* That is a higher kind of rest than the other; it is only given to those that take the yoke of Jesus and learn of Him.

In the seventh verse we have a very sweet expression: *"When Boaz had eaten and drunk, and his heart was merry."* Do you know why? Eating and drinking means satisfying. He was satisfied. If the chaff had been winnowed away, he was satisfied with what was left. *"He shall see the travail of His soul, and shall be satisfied"* (Isa. 53:11). Christ will experience that in most of His Church, by-and-by, at the end of the harvest. The harvest was over, the barley was winnowed, and the master was happy. And Boaz said,

> *"Tarry this night, and it shall be in the morning, that if he will perform unto thee the part of a kinsman, well; let him do the kinsman's part: but if he will not do the part of a kinsman to thee, then will I do the part of a kinsman to thee as the LORD liveth: lie down until the morning"* (v. 13).

What a sweet advice that was: *"Lie down until the morning."*

In the second chapter we read that *"she gleaned in the field until even."* What a contrast now that she is at the feet of Boaz! Those two verses put together, make the Christian's work down here: *"Glean until even"*; *"lie down until the morning."* That which is going to be morning to the Church is going to be night to the world. Those who rest at the Master's feet will do the most work.

> *"Also he said, 'Bring the vail that thou hast upon thee and hold it. And when she held it, he measured six measures of barley, and laid it on her; and she went into the city"* (v. 15).

Notice what she got for resting. Better than ever she got for gleaning. Then she got an ephah of barley and a lot of straw. The servant gave her that, but Boaz never gives any straw. It was barley he gave her; there was nothing to beat out. It was winnowed barley. If you trust the Master, and work for Him, you will get more in five minutes than you would in ten years if you work for yourself.

She received six measures of barley. Why not seven? Seven is the complete or perfect number. I will tell you why. He was going to give her the seventh measure in the morning. You know what that was—it was himself. There is nothing perfect here. Even the Master does not give us perfection now; but when the morning comes we will have Him! Without Him there is nothing perfect, nothing complete. When Boaz gave Ruth the barley, he measured it; but afterward, when she got himself, she got all the barley too, without measure. Our blessings are measured today, but in the morning we will get them all.

> *"When she came to her mother-in-law, she told her all that the man had done to her. And she said 'These six measures of barley gave he me; for he said to me, go not empty unto thy mother-in-law"* (vv. 16-17).

It would have been a downright shame for her to have gone home from the presence of Boaz empty. And there is no reason for us to be empty. Yet how empty we are sometimes! We talk, when we might as well have been silent. They are idle words, and nothing more. We may talk about the Saviour as clearly and logically as Paul did, and yet be empty. Do you know why? Because we have not been at the Master's feet. None that ever came to the Master and trusted Him went empty away. The reason why much of our testimony is useless is because we have trusted ourselves, our brain, or some book, or some kind of knowledge we possess, instead of going to the feet of Christ, and learning of Him; you shall have the grandest day tomorrow you ever had, if you will spend today at the feet of the Master. What a difference it makes, going full and going empty.

I was in New York some time ago, and a friend told me he had been at a meeting where he spoke to a girl who had been rescued from a life of sin. He asked her how she became a Christian. She told him how she had once lived in a certain place, one of the vile dens of New York. She fell sick there, and was neglected by everybody. One day, however, a knock came to the door, and a young lady entered the room. She saw how things were, and she said to the sick girl, "Would you like me to put the bed straight, and sweep the floor, and kindle the fire for you?" She let her do it, and afterwards said, "She was kind to me, and spoke some passages of Scripture; and when she went away she said, 'Good bye.' But I did not feel the slightest impression on my heart from what she had said. She came again the next day, and the next. She was very kind; she brought me food, and did all she could. She never went away without giving me a text of Scripture, yet it did not make any impression.

"One day she came and straightened up my room, and made my bed. Just as she was going away, she came to the bedside, and looked at me. She put her hand on my brow, and said, 'God bless you, my child, God bless you!' and she stooped and kissed me. It was that kiss that opened my heart."

This young lady had gone full of the spirit of her Master; the result was, she took some winnowed barley, and that poor soul was saved.

My sister, my brother, go from the presence of the Master to your work. Take with you the winnowed barley He has given you. Thank God, He has given you six measures; take it to the starving and the dying, and He will bless you. We shall be as happy as the Lord Jesus Christ wants us to be, if we only do what He wants us to do. May He bless His simple message to your soul!

Chapter 4
Ruth Rewarded

You will have noticed in the third chapter, Boaz said to Ruth, that in the morning he would consult one who had the first claim upon her—the first kinsman, who was nearer than himself. And at last the morning has come. So Boaz went up to the gate, and the first kinsman came by. Boaz said to him: *"Sit down here."* Then in the second verse of this chapter we read, that Boaz

> *"Took ten men of the elders of the city, and said, 'Sit ye down here'; and they sat down."*

You find there were three questions to be settled. The first was this: Was there a kinsmen who had **the right** to redeem? The second: Was there a kinsman who was **able** to redeem? And thirdly: Was there a kinsman who was **willing** to redeem? These three things were necessary.

First of all the man must have **the right.** You or I might be as rich as Baron Rothschild, yet we could not have redeemed the inheritance, because we were not kinsmen. And so, was there not a necessity for the Lord Jesus Christ becoming man, in order that He might be our kinsman? It was only as man that He had a right to redeem.

Then the next thing was: Had he **the ability** to do it? Suppose Boaz had been poor instead of rich, he might have had the right, and he might have wanted to redeem the inheritance; but if he had not been able it would have been an impossibility. But we are told that he was a *"mighty man of wealth,"* so that he had not only the right, but the ability to redeem.

Then there was **the willingness** of the redeemer. He might have had the right, he might have had the means; but if he had not the heart, no power on earth could have made Boaz redeem the inheritance, and redeem poor Ruth. That is why we read so much in Scripture about the **love** of Christ. It was not the

pity of Christ; it took something more than pity. It was not the **sympathy** of Christ; it took something more than sympathy. It took nothing less than the **love** of Christ to become our Saviour and Redeemer.

Then notice the two kinsmen stand there, and the ten elders are the witnesses. Boaz said to the first kinsman: *"Elimelech had a piece of land, and Naomi selleth it. Will you redeem it?"* Yes, he said, he would. *"Well, along with it there is Ruth, the Moabitess; will you take her along with the land?"* No, he said, "I cannot take her; I will take the property, but I will have nothing to do with her."

But, though the first kinsman would not redeem Ruth, there is no disagreement between the two; they are not contrary the one to the other.

> *"Redeem thou my right to thyself; for I cannot redeem it"* (v. 6).

Between law and grace, while there is the greatest contrast, thank God there is no antagonism. God's justice and God's love work in parallel lines.

The next thing is, Boaz has got the whole people together, and he takes hold of this poor Gentile girl. He calls the people to witness – that he is going to give her – some parched corn? No. To drop some handfuls of purpose? No. The morning had come and he was going to fulfill his promise to her. Ruth had done everything he had told her. From first to last you find Ruth in the path of obedience; so she is always satisfied. The most dissatisfied people on the earth are Christians who are disobedient to the command of Christ. They go seeking pleasure, and they cannot find it. They go into the world looking for joy. Beloved, there is a plant that never blossomed in this world, and that is the plant of joy, the plant of happiness. It only grows where the Master is; it does not grow in the world at all. That is why nobody in the world is satisfied. They are looking forward from the beginning to the end of "the season," and from one season to another, but it finds them exactly where they were, unsatisfied. If you had the whole world at your feet today, and had not got Christ, you would not be satisfied. And if you had Christ, and were not walking in the path of obedience, you would still be most wretched.

But the morning has come, and Ruth is going to get the fullness of the blessing which Boaz intended for her. What was that? One of Boaz' fields? No, not that. A beautiful cottage upon his estate? Not that. How many Christians say: "I shall be glad to get one of the many mansions: I shall be glad to get inside the gate." But that did not satisfy Ruth. She took whatever Boaz gave her. If it was only *"handfuls of purpose,"* she took that. But now he is going to give **himself** to her. And so faith takes all that Jehovah gives; and the greatest gift is Himself.

The morning came at last. Notice what Boaz does. He takes that poor Gentile girl, who had not a shilling in the world, and before all the people says:

> *"Ye are witness ... Ruth, the Moabitess, I have purchased to be my wife"* (v. 9-10).

The richest man in the land takes a beggar and says, "I have purchased her to make her my wife!"

What is the hope of the Church – your hope and mine? A mansion? Thank God there is something better than a mansion. Golden streets and jasper walls? No! It is the blessed Master Himself! Grace would never be satisfied with giving us a mansion, a beautiful home. Christ gives nothing less than **Himself.** *"Who loved me, and gave **Himself** for me."*

Turn to a few passages of Scripture on the coming back of our blessed Lord according to His promise, because this subject leads us right to it. The morning is sure to come, and it cannot be very long now. I think the Church is almost at day-break now; looking at the state of the world, I think it is very near the time when the Son of God will come back again. You need not be alarmed; I am not going to speak about seals being broken, or of trumpets being blown, or of vials being emptied. I am not going into these things, because I do not understand them myself. Thank God, He has given us a very simple revelation in His Word, and that is the return of the Son of God from heaven to receive His Church.

Turn to the 14th chapter of John's Gospel. That is the first place I can find in the four Gospels, where the Saviour speaks about His return. Those who have studied this subject will bear in mind two things; it will help you a great deal. In passages where you read *"the day of the Lord,"* it does not mean the coming of the Lord Jesus Christ for His Church. If you begin at Isaiah 4, and go right through the Old Testament you will find *"the day of the Lord"* mentioned by almost every prophet. Trace it also in the New Testament, and you will find *"the day of the Lord"* means the day of judgement by the Lord Jesus Christ upon the nations that have persecuted the Jews. You never find one place where the coming of the Lord is mentioned in connection with anything but the hope of the Church. People are always associating the coming of the Lord with judgement. I will tell you something that may surprise you. Not a single believer in the Lord Jesus Christ in this dispensation will ever be in the judgement at all. We shall be **at** the judgement but not **in** the judgement. *"Know ye not that the saints shall judge the world?"* There is a great difference between judging and being judged.

Now, notice in the 13th chapter of John, the Lord Jesus Christ has gathered His disciples together away from the world, that He might tell them some secrets. And, first, He tells them that they must have their feet washed. And then another thing was, they were to love one another. That was before a single word was said about the Master's coming back again.

Then in the 14th chapter, He begins by saying, *"Let not your heart be troubled."* He does not say, "Let not your **hearts** be troubled," but your **heart.** God never makes any mistakes about His language. You or I would never have talked about *"your heart."* There were eleven of them. Why does He say heart? Because they had got their feet washed, and loved one another, and they are all of one heart. *"I go to prepare a place for you. And if I go and prepare a place for you, I will come again, and receive you unto Myself."* I want you to notice that little word *"receive."* It is not, I am coming to **take** you, but to **receive** you. I remember once quoting that passage in Ireland—that is a place where they read their Bibles a good deal. A lady came to me and asked me to show her where it was said that Christ would take His disciples to Himself. I turned to this verse and read, *"I will come again and receive you unto Myself."* "But you said **take**; it is not take at all, but **receive**!"

There is a wonderful lesson to be learned here. If I am going to receive anything, I must receive it **from** somebody. And so it seems to me, that when the Lord Jesus Christ comes back again, the Holy Spirit takes up the Church, and presents it to the Master.

Well, some people say: "I believe in Christ's coming back because I cannot deny that it is taught in the word." But they try to explain away His personal coming. "Yes," they say, "the Lord Jesus Christ said He would come back again, but it means at death." That it does not, I think I can prove to you. Death is an enemy of the Lord Jesus Christ. Death is an enemy of the Church; it is not a friend, and our Lord will not send an enemy in place of Himself.

Our Lord said: *"I will come again Myself."* Then some people say: "Oh, yes, but He meant Titus coming to Jerusalem; that was the coming of the Lord." The idea of an old heathen idolater being Christ! "Well then," say others, "it meant this; the gradual spread of the Gospel all over the world. The Gospel is to be preached, and people are going to be saved. It meant a spiritual coming." No, it does not mean that. You cannot find a passage from the beginning of Matthew to the end of the book of Revelation, where it says that the world is going to be made better, and better, and better by the preaching of the Gospel – not a solitary passage. But the Book tells me that the world is going to get worse, and worse, and worse! That the Lord Jesus Christ is gathering out His Church, and after He has gathered out His elect, He is going to return and take that Church away, while the world will be left to go on in its sin and iniquity, just as at this present time.

"Well then," they say, "it means that when I am converted the Lord comes into my soul; that is what is meant by the coming of the Lord." The apostle Paul said, *"Christ lives in me,"* and it was only after his conversion that he could write that. Yet it was **after that** he began to speak about the Lord's coming again, not before. If the Lord had come back to Paul, he would have told us; but he did not, therefore it cannot mean that. Suppose you have got a son in a foreign land, and he writes to you, "Dear mother, I am coming back by the next ship. All being well, I hope to be home by such and such a day." Who would you expect to come back? Some shadow? Some peculiar kind of feeling round your heart? Would you say that was your son come back? No! You would expect a carriage to drive up to the door, and that your boy would get out, and nobody else. So when Christ said, *"I will come again,"* He just meant Himself. He did not mean a spirit or an influence. He did not mean somebody else; He meant **Himself.**

Now turn to Acts 1:9-11:

> *"And when He had spoken these things, while they beheld, He was taken up; and a cloud received Him out of their sight. And while they looked steadfastly towards heaven as He went up, behold two men stood by them in white apparel; which also said, 'Ye men of Galilee, why stand ye gazing up into heaven? This same Jesus, which is taken up from you into heaven, shall so come in like manner, as ye have seen Him go into heaven.'"* Notice these words, because they are very important. *"In like manner as ye have seen Him go into heaven."*

These angels understood what Jesus meant far better than the people who write commentaries. They came right down from heaven to tell us, and they said, *"Just as He has gone, He is to come again."* How did He go? In the last chapter of Luke, we read how He went. Verse 39: *"A spirit hath not flesh and bones, as you see Me have."* It was not a spirit that went away, but the very same Jesus who died on the cross and came out of the tomb.

> *"And He led them out as far as Bethany. And He lifted up His hands and blessed them. And it came to pass, while He blessed them, He was parted from them, and carried*

up into heaven" (vv. 50-51).

What a sweet sight it must have been! I used to wonder why He went to Bethany. When the Lord Jesus Christ was down here, He did not know many friends. There were not many of those rich Pharisees who asked Him to go and sleep in their homes.

But at Bethany lived two sisters, Martha and Mary, with their brother Lazarus, and whenever Jesus went there He was welcome. They were always glad to see Him in their humble home. Now He is going away. And you know when you are going a long distance, you nearly always go and see your particular friends to bid them good-bye. So I think He went to Bethany – I have no Scripture for it, but it is my opinion – just to bid Lazarus, and Martha, and Mary, good-bye, to tell them He was going back to His Father, but He would come back again for them by-and-by.

"He led them out as far as to Bethany and blessed them." The last words that ever came from the dear Saviour's lips were words of blessing to His Church. And He is coming back in the same way; not to curse His Church, but to bless her. *"He lifted up His hands."* The last thing they saw were those pierced hands. As much as if He had said: "Peter, James, John, Nathaniel, never forget that I have been crucified for you; never forget that the nails have been through My hands, and My feet, and the spear in My side. Whatever you do, keep out of the world, for it has murdered Me. Do not go and live for its pleasures, its sins and its folly; but come out and be separate." Oh, friend, if the Son of God came back today, would He find you in the world? Do you care about its applause? The world is a hollow bubble, and you know it, you have experienced it. And the last thing the Master says to you is: "I have been crucified for you, not only to bring you to heaven, but to deliver you from this present evil world." May God help His Church to be separate, and to live for Him!

Now turn to 2 Corinthians 5:1-6, where we have another sweet thought in connection with our Lord's return.

> *"For we know that if our earthly house of this tabernacle were dissolved, we have a building of God, a house not*

made with hands, eternal in the heavens. For in this we groan, earnestly desiring to be clothed upon with our house which is from heaven; if so be that being clothed we shall not be found naked. For we that are in this tabernacle do groan, being burdened; not for that we would be unclothed, but clothed upon, that mortality might be swallowed up of life. Now He that hath wrought us for the self same thing is God, who also hath given unto us the earnest of the Spirit. Therefore we are always confident, knowing that whilst we are at home in the body, we are absent from the Lord."

Paul was just a glorious subject of the Master. He had got the right idea in his brain, and that was, that there was something better to live for than all this world could give—and heaven besides. That was the Lord Jesus Christ Himself. He did not talk much about the mansions; he talked about the Lord, **the Lord, THE LORD!** You find it so all through these epistles. It was not the golden streets, the beautiful throne, the white robes or the crown; but the Lord Himself.

When I was in Rochester, New York, some time ago, friends wanted to send a doll to my little daughter, a crippled, paralyzed child of five years; so they got a very pretty doll for her. I wrote to her: "Dear Minnie, I am going to bring you such a pretty doll." I had a letter back to say that Minnie wanted me to come home as soon as I could with the doll; every other letter was about the doll.

So it happened that I had to come home by another ship than the one I expected to go by, so the doll went by a different ship, and did not reach there till three or four weeks after I had been home. When I arrived I sat down, and Minnie sat on the hearth-rug. By-and-by she said: "Papa, will it be long before you unpack your trunk?" I said, "No, I do not think it will be very long." My heart began to fail me, because I thought it was the only the doll she wanted, but I sat still. Presently she said: "Papa, I **would** like to help you unpack your boxes." I could not hide it any longer, so I said, "Well, Minnie, I am sorry to have to tell you that after all I had to leave your doll in America; I have come without it." In a moment that sweet little girl looked up at me with her pretty eyes, and she said: "Papa, I would rather have you than the doll!" I could not tell you how it gladdened me to hear her say that; it cheered me to know that after all, she wanted me to come back, not for what I was going to give, but for myself. And we do not want our Lord back again for the gifts He is going to bestow. We want **Him** back again because we love Him. It is our blessed Lord and Master Himself that we long for.

Now turn to Philippians 3:20; 1 Thessalonians 1:9-10:

> *"For our conversation is in heaven; from whence also we look for the Saviour, the Lord Jesus Christ." ... "For they themselves show us what manner of entering in we had unto you, and how ye turned to God from idols to serve the living and true God, and to wait for His Son from heaven, whom He raised from the dead, even Jesus, which delivered us from the wrath to come."*

I want you to notice that these people to whom the apostle wrote, had not got any more intellect than you and I have. People say we cannot understand what is meant here. Why, do you think these poor heathens who had just been rescued from idolatry understood it? They believed it, whether they understood it or not. And so God wants us to believe, even if we do not understand. The question is, is it true? God has said it; let us believe it, whether we understand it or not.

I sometimes wonder what those people in the church at Thessalonica would have thought if Paul, after he had told them all about the coming of the Saviour, had written again, "My dear brethren, I know you cannot understand anything that I have written you. I would advise you to buy a commentary in order to have my epistle explained to you!" What would they have said? They just believed that they were to *"wait for His Son from heaven."* And that is what they were doing. They were waiting; not discussing, not arguing, not trying to bring out different opinions. They had *"turned to God from idols to serve the living and true God."* Mark you, they did not lie on couches and say, *"We are waiting."* They served Him. The people who are working for Christ are the people who are waiting for Him. If you are waiting for Him, you will work for Him too, there is no doubt about that.

> *"But I would not have you to be ignorant, brethren, concerning them which are asleep, that ye sorrow not, even as others, which have no hope. For if we believe that Jesus died and rose again, even so them also which sleep in Jesus will God bring with Him"* (1 Thess. 4:13-14).

These are sweet words, *"them also which sleep in Jesus."* There is no mother who is afraid when her little boy is asleep in the cradle. The Lord has just hushed our loved ones quietly to rest. They are asleep. But He is coming to wake them up by-and-by. Then the apostle says, *"For this we say unto you,* ***by the Word of the Lord****"* (v. 15). Not by opinion of some great commentator, but *"by the Word of the Lord," "that we which are alive and remain unto the coming of the Lord shall not prevent them which are asleep.* ***For the Lord Himself****"*—not angels, not archangels, not the multitude of spirits, but *"the Lord Himself."*

Our Bridegroom is coming Himself, He is not going to send any one else. *"The Lord Himself shall descent from heaven with a shout,"*—that is, a shout of victory (v. 16). *"With the voice of the archangel,"*—the only place in which you read of an archangel speaking, is when he was contending about the body of Moses (Jude 9). He is coming back to claim our bodies. How is He going to raise those bodies that have gone to dust? Suppose I were thrown overboard in the middle of the Atlantic and was swallowed up by fishes; how is the Lord to raise my body? I do not know, and I do not care. That is not my business. I have only to believe that He is going to raise it, because He says so. We have nothing to do with the "how."

> *"And the dead in Christ shall rise first: then we which are alive and remain shall be caught up together with them in the clouds, to meet the Lord in the air and so shall we ever be with the Lord. Wherefore comfort one another with these words"* (1 Thess. 4:17-18).

Now turn to Revelation 22:20: *"He which testifieth these things saith, 'Surely I come quickly. Amen.' Even so come, Lord Jesus."* The last telegram that ever came from heaven said, *"Surely, I come quickly."* Another telegram is sent back, *"Even so, come, Lord Jesus."* How that ought to comfort us! How, every day, instead of getting sadder and more sorrowful, we ought to get fuller of joy, of life, and light, and happiness! Do you know the happiest day of your life? Not the day you were converted. It ought to be **today**. And why? Because you are so much nearer being with the Bridegroom—so much nearer being with the blessed Saviour.

A few years ago I was in Philadelphia. I was going to a place in Pennsylvania. As I entered the railway car, I noticed a foreign-looking woman, with a peculiar kind of handkerchief on her head. There was a little girl with her, who also had this peculiar sort of handkerchief on her head. They began to talk together in some strange language. I thought to myself: "What a sorrowful looking woman she is! I wanted to try and comfort her; but we could not understand each other. She looked so wretched. By-and-by the whistle sounded, and the train started away.

After we had got about ten miles, she put her hand into her pocket, took out a letter and began to read it. Presently she said something to the little girl, and I saw for a moment, just a little smile upon her face; then it faded away and she was as sad as ever. After the train had gone about fifty miles, I turned and looked, and I thought at that moment I saw her smile. A little further on I looked again, and she really did smile. I was quite sure I caught a smile on her face. Further on I heard her talking away to the little girl: she had got the letter in her hand, and she actually laughed!

By-and-by we came to a station and she immediately put up the window and looked out; she said something and shook her head. Then at every station I noticed that up went the window, and she looked as if she would see some one. By-and-by we came to a station, and she was just putting up the window when she saw somebody. He gave a cry: she gave a cry, and the next minute the door swung open, and a big man ran right to her and kissed her. He looked at the little girl and kissed her too. Oh, there was joy then! She had met her loved one; the child had met the father, and the wife her husband, and there was joy. Every mile of the journey she knew would bring her nearer to the one she loved best on earth, and when they met at last how happy she seemed! The train started away, and by-and-by we came to another station. As we drew near—I fancy I can see him now—he took his wife and the little girl by the hand to the opposite side of the car, and pointed to a beautiful cottage with green shutters and a nice garden in the front. As they walked back, she put her arms around his neck and kissed him again. I suppose he was saying: "That is the house that I have got ready for you; is it not pretty? We shall never be separated again."

Beloved, we have got a letter from One who is coming for us. We know not the day or the hour when He may come, but I think we are very near the time when He will return for His loved ones. Then our dear friends will be raised again, and we shall be with them. Then we shall be forever with the Lord.

Brother, sister, father, mother, is it not worth while living a life of self-denial down here? Is it not worth while saying to the world: "Stand aside; I will have nothing to do with thee, but to witness against thy evil deeds!" Just for one single smile from the lips of that blessed Bridegroom, and to hear Him say: *"Well done, thou good and faithful servant, enter thou into the joy of thy Lord!"* Mother, He is coming back: are you living for Him? Sister, He is coming back: are you living for Him? Father, brother, are you living for Him?

Just imagine Ruth, in all her poverty, being ashamed to own her bridegroom; ashamed to own Boaz, the mighty man of wealth, who had rescued her from that life of poverty, and who was not satisfied to give her anything but himself, and with himself all that he had!

Oh, never be ashamed of Christ; never be ashamed of that blessed Lord who may come back today! Then, when He appears, you will never have the privilege of doing what you can do today—of living for Christ, and not for self.

May God bless these simple readings, and may He by His Spirit teach us to love this blessed Bible because it tells us, from first to last, about the Lord Jesus Christ. May God add His blessing for Christ's sake.

Ambassadors for Christ

"Now then we are ambassadors for Christ, as though God did beseech you by us: we pray you in Christ's stead, be ye reconciled to God" (2 Cor. 5:20).

What is it to be an ambassador? I was crossing the Atlantic in a steamship a little time ago; and there was on board a gentleman who had been an ambassador from the United States to Russia. He told me a great many things about ambassadors that I never knew before.

First of all, an ambassador is never sent to his own country, but to a foreign land. The United States had sent their ambassador to Europe, and, said he, "I felt I was a stranger there all the time." It is so with the Christian; we are not at home down here, whatever people may think about it. If we are ambassadors for Christ, we are *"strangers and pilgrims"* in this world. Another thing this gentleman told me. He said: "We are never sent as ambassadors to a country that we are at war with. If there were to be a war between the United States and Russia, a telegraphic message would come and call me home again. There would be no war as long as our ambassador remained there." And so there is no war between God and the world as long as He has got ambassadors here. The very fact that God had got ambassadors here is a proof that God is at peace with the world and not at war. When He calls all the ambassadors home, then judgement will come, but not till then. We preach peace through the Lord Jesus Christ. And it is a sweet thought that the Saviour is coming again by-and-by, that He is going to receive us to be with Himself forever.

Something else I learned. Supposing my country were going to send an ambassador to this land, we should select some one in whom we had confidence. But suppose the one who was chosen said, "I do not like crossing the Atlantic; I will go over to Valentia in Ireland, which is the nearest point to America, and there I will build a beautiful castle. If these Americans want to have anything to say to me, they must come over to where I am." Why, if he were to say that, we should not send him. But there are a great many people who act in that way. They say, "Oh, yes; we will give something to help to build a mission or a church, and if people like to come to it, why, they can. It is here, and if they do not like to come, then it is their business." My friend, there is not a single passage of scripture that tells an unconverted man to go to church at all. The ambassador to America has to leave his country and come to Washington. And if we are ambassadors for Christ, it is not for us to tell the world to come to us, but it is our privilege and our duty to go to the world and tell them the Gospel of our Lord Jesus Christ.

Something else about ambassadors. The world judges of the Lord Jesus Christ by what they see in us. If you were to go to a foreign country as the representative of your land, they would look at you, and from you they would form a judgement of what your people are. Not very long since a friend of mine told me that one of the smartest lawyers in the State of Illinois—or Indiana, I forget which—was sent as ambassador to Austria. After he had been there some little time, he took to drinking, and died of delirium tremens. My friend said that in Austria, to this day, they believe the Americans are the most drunken nation on the face of the earth, because their ambassador died of delirium tremens. The world cannot see the Master, and so they judge of Christianity by what they see in those who call themselves Christians.

The ambassador has got a message, and it is a very simple one. People say they cannot tell the Gospel of Christ. I am sure they could if they tried. Christ's message to John was simply to go and say, "Come;" anybody can say, "Come." "Oh, yes," some people say, "but we have not got the gift." There is no human soul who has not got a greater gift than any angel in heaven. There is not angel in heaven can do what you can do—tell a poor sinner about the precious blood of the Lord Jesus Christ. Instead of looking to Christ, and His power and willingness to help, a great many people are continually looking to themselves.

I remember taking tea with a friend, Mr. Smithies, in Dublin, some years ago, and he told me a little incident which made a great impression on my mind, and which I have never forgotten. There had been a flower show somewhere, and many flowers had been sent to compete for prizes. There was one beautiful geranium which took the prize; and when the judges came to give out the prizes, this one was claimed by the poor little girl who lived away in the east of London. The judges could scarcely believe that the plant belonged to her. She told her story and it was something like this: The flower had been given to her when it was very small, and they told her it could not live unless it had plenty of water and sunshine. She said the sun did not shine much in the court where she lived, but she got up early in the morning, and put her flower in the sun; and as the sun went around, she moved her plant, so as to keep it in the sunshine. And she won the prize. Our gift may be very small, but if we keep it in the sunshine it is sure to grow. We want to get near and keep near the Sun of Righteousness. If we do, our little gift will develop, and we may gain a prize by-and-by, which others with a greater talent than ours may miss, because they did not keep their gift in the sunshine.

Our message is one of reconciliation. We are to beseech sinners—to pray them—to be reconciled to God. I want to put it to you solemnly. Have you been faithful, honest, and true to your ambassadorship? Let us imagine that there is a man in prison who is condemned to be executed for murder. The Governor sends for me, and I go to his office. He asks me if I would like to take a message of pardon to the condemned man. "Yes," I say, "I should very much like to do so." "Here it is," says he; "but that man is very obstinate, and I want you to go and beseech him to take the pardon from me." So I get the pardon. It is beautifully signed and sealed, and I put it in my pocket. I come back to the city and I jump into a carriage. On the way, I stop at a shop where there are some beautiful flowers, and there I purchase a handsome bouquet. A little further on I stop the driver again, at a shop where they sell music. "Have you any nice new songs—something nice and soothing?" "Yes, some very nice ones." "Give me half a dozen." So, with the music in one hand and the flowers in the other, I drive to the prison. I show my credentials, and I get into the condemned cell. I have not long to stop—some twenty or thirty minutes, perhaps, is all I am allowed. "My friend," I say to the man, "I have got something for you; I have been to the Governor's office." "Have you?" "Yes; it is a beautiful place." And I begin to tell him about it, about the nice pictures, the fine carpets, and about the Governor, and how kind he was, and how nicely he spoke, and so on. But he does not seem to care much about it. "I have new songs. Would you like to hear me sing?" So I sing two or three of these nice songs. By-and-by, as I am finishing the singing, the key is put into the lock; the lock turns, the door opens; the turnkey says, "You cannot stay any longer," and I have to leave the prison. All the time I have got the pardon in my pocket, and I never said a word to him about it. I entertained him nicely, but never told him of the message—never begged him, prayed him, pleaded with him to receive the pardon. What would you think about me? Would you not say that his blood was upon these hands?

Brethren, what have you done with the pardon? Is it in your pocket? You have got a beautiful Bagster's Bible, nicely bound and marked, and you say, "How nice it is!" But what about the pardon? What about the message? What about praying, beseeching, entreating sinners to be reconciled to God? In the Master's name I ask you, as ambassadors for Christ, have you been honest and faithful, and true to your Master and your God? To how many souls have you spoken today about the Saviour's love? My friend, it is not beautiful entertainments that sinners want; it is the Gospel of the Lord Jesus Christ. Just think what a power there is in the message! You say, "I have spoken sometimes, and it did not seem to produce any impression." **How** did you speak? God has told us in this beautiful verse—pray, beseech, entreat. We may speak in such a way as to drive sinners away from Christ, but we may also speak so as to draw them to the Saviour. Try a tear. There is power in a tear—or a kind word. Go in the Master's name, and speak as He would speak, words of love; hearts are sure to break then. A little time ago I was in New York, and a friend was telling me about a meeting she had attended. Some twenty or thirty ladies met for prayer in connection with the work of trying to rescue some of the poor fallen ones. There was a young girl sitting there, with her face almost as bright as an angel; she had only been converted a little while, and she said she would like to tell about it. She lived in one of the very bad streets in New York. She was taken ill. No one came near her; she had been left alone for two or three days, when one day a knock came to the door, and a young lady came in. "I have heard about you," she said to her sick sister, "and I have some to see if I can help you." She got up and swept the room, lighted the stove, smoothed the invalid's pillow, and said she would come again. When she went away, she repeated Scripture, but it did not make any impression on the sick one. She came again, did up the little room, and went away, repeating a text; still it made no impression. She came for several days, and one day she came, swept up the floor, cooked some dinner, and made everything look nice. "Then," continued the narrator, "she came and looked at me, and put her hand on my brow, and stooping down, she kissed me. As she kissed me I saw a tear trickling down her face. It was that kiss that did it."

I tell you friends, that is what we want—to speak as if we meant and believed what this blessed Book teaches. We are *"ambassadors for Christ."* May God help us to do the Master's work in the Master's way—to speak as we think He would speak, to work as we think He would work! He has given us the glorious privilege of being His representatives down here; may we use that privilege to His glory!

Bible Readings
The Good Shepherd

"I am the Good Shepherd" (John 10:11).

I want to ask our friends to take their Bibles, and turn with me to a few passages of Scripture in connection with the subject of the Lord Jesus Christ as **the Good Shepherd**.

You remember that in John 10, the Saviour calls Himself the *"Good Shepherd"*; and you know He told us that His mission down here was to teach us about God His Father. It was not very often He spoke about Himself; but when He did, it was something to cheer and encourage His people. Now, the Lord Jesus tells us twice over in this wonderful chapter that He is the Good Shepherd; and we know that whatever the Saviour said He meant—therefore, when He tells us He is the Good Shepherd, we know that He is so, simply because He said it. But we shall find it very profitable to take God's Word, and see for ourselves what the Good Shepherd has done for us, is doing for us, and will do for us.

All these little details we find brought out so sweetly in God's blessed Word.

The first shepherd was Abel, though he was not called a shepherd, that term being afterward used. God called him a *"keeper of sheep"*; **shepherd** means simply a **keeper of sheep**. My friends, some Christians imagine that perhaps, after all, they may perish; but no, they cannot; a shepherd is not a loser, but a **keeper** of sheep. The Lord is the Good Shepherd, and will not lose us, but means to keep us.

The word *"shepherd"* is first used in Genesis 46:32, in connection with Jacob and his family coming down to Joseph; and we read (v. 34) that they went to dwell in the land of Goshen, *"for every shepherd is an abomination to the Egyptians."* But more: in Exodus 8:26, we find that sheep also were an abomination to the Egyptians; so that the shepherd and the sheep were both detested by them. Yes, and they have not changed yet. We are the sheep, and Christ is the Shepherd, both being abominable to the world. If you want to go into the world as one of Christ's fold, the world will not have you; worldlings do not want the Master, and they do not want His sheep. Go to them as a worldly man, and you are all right; go as a child of God, and you are all wrong. There is another noticeable thing in connection with the shepherd. The sheep were entrusted to him, and were required back from him. You remember what Jacob said to Laban concerning any that were missing from the flock: *"I bare the loss; of my hand didst thou require it."* But not a single sheep of the Lord Jesus can be lost, because He is the Good Shepherd, and has given His life for the sheep. Now, let us read Ezekiel 34:11-16, and see what the Shepherd has done for the sheep:

> *"For thus saith the Lord God; 'Behold I, even I, will both search My sheep, and seek them out. As a shepherd seeketh out his flock in the day that he is among his sheep that are scattered, so will I seek out My sheep, and will deliver them out of all places where they have been scattered in the cloudy and dark day. And I will bring them out from the people, and gather them from the countries, and will bring them to their own land, and feed them upon the mountains of Israel by the rivers, and in all the inhabited places of the country. I will fed them in a good pasture, and upon the high mountain of Israel shall their fold be; there shall they lie in a good fold, and in a fat pasture shall they feed upon the mountains of Israel. I will feed My flock, and I will cause them to lie down,' saith the Lord God. 'I will seek that which was lost, and bring again that which was driven away; and will bind up that which was broken, and will strengthen that which was sick; but I will destroy the fat and the strong; I will feed them with judgement.'"*

I want you to observe **six** things in this passage that the Shepherd promises to do for the sheep: and mark, He says, "I" will do them. He will do them Himself, and not through another.

I will **seek** them,
I will **deliver** them,
I will **separate** them,
I will **bring them to their own land**,
I will **satisfy** them,
I will **make them rest**.

Eighteen hundred years ago, the Lord Jesus came to seek and to save that which was lost; and He is doing it now. He found us in the house of bondage, in captivity, and He delivered us; He died not only to save us, but to separate us by His own precious blood, from a guilty world; then He will bring us to our own land, and there will He feed us. It is striking that He never promises to feed the sheep until they get their own land. God did not send the manna till the people had left Egypt; the prodigal son did not see his father till he left the far country. He will feed us; and you know feeding means satisfying. You cannot get a sheep to lie down until you have fed it—until it is satisfied; and the Shepherd says, "I will feed and satisfy you, and cause you to lie down to rest."

Now turn to another passage, to which I am sure our minds go at once—Psalm 23. I suppose nearly every one can repeat this Psalm from memory; but every one cannot repeat it from the heart. I will tell you why. There is not a sheep in the fold of Christ that can say it from the heart unless that sheep is satisfied; then he can lie down. Some are always seeking some one to satisfy them, but will not let the Master do it; yet non can satisfy, except the Good Shepherd Himself, and He will. Until we come to Him, we can find nothing to satisfy.

I want to call your attention to the three Psalms brought together here very sweetly—Psalms 22, 23 and 24. They should never be read separately. You know in John, Jesus is called the Good Shepherd, because He laid down His life for the sheep: in Hebrews, He is called the Great Shepherd, because He is risen from the dead: in Peter, He is called the Chief Shepherd, because He is coming back again. There is **Death, Resurrection** and the **Second Coming** of Christ, in connection with His sheep. And if you will read this beautiful 22nd Psalm, you will find the Good Shepherd giving His life for them; in the 23rd, you have the Great Shepherd in the resurrection blessing them; and in the 24th you find the Chief Shepherd leading them through the pearly gates into the better land. There is the Good, the Great and the Chief Shepherd.

"The LORD is my Shepherd." He must not be only **our** Shepherd, but **my** Shepherd. And dismal and dark as are many places around us, there is not one poor, wretched creature but can – if he but believes on the Lord Jesus—say as much as David, *"The LORD is my Shepherd."* Yes, thank God, if we are in His fellowship, we can say individually, *"My Shepherd; I shall not want."* Then He says, *"He maketh me to lie down in green pastures,"* etc. You know we sometimes see sheep driven along the dusty road, and you see them wearied and tired; afterward, they get a little grass, and the poor things are allowed to rest. That is not the way our Shepherd deals with us. He does not drive us till we are tired, and then feed us. It is not leading and then resting; but rest first and leading next.

But more, *"He restoreth my soul."* I wondered why the restoring came in there; but it is because the nearer we are to Him, the more Satan will tempt us. He will try to draw our hearts away; but the Shepherd puts out His right hand and restores us. Sheep must be near the Shepherd to be restored, and they must be near him to be tempted.

Now, I want to notice particularly this 4th verse, because it is one of the sweetest in Scripture: *"Yea though I walk through the valley of the shadow of death, I will fear no evil: for Thou art with me; Thy rod and Thy staff they comfort me."*

I believe the *"valley of the shadow of death"* means not only the shadow that is on everything around us here, but when passing through death itself, if the Lord tarries. And notice a wonderful change here. In the 2nd and 3rd verses, it is *"He"*; but now, in the 4th, it is no longer *"He."* As soon as we get into the valley, there is something sweeter. You may talk **of** Him, but there is something better than that; in the valley we talk **to** Him. *"For **Thou*** *art with me."* Is there not something very sweet and precious in that beautiful word, **Thou**? Have we not noticed, again and again, as we sat by the death-bed of some one that loved the Master, that after the eye is closed and they do not recognize us, when the ear is shut and they cannot hear our voice, have you not seen a beautiful glow steal across their face, and the lips moving as if conversing with some one? It was not to us, it was not to an angel. To whom were they speaking? Was it not the Good Shepherd? Yes, my brother; yes, my sister; if you have to enter that valley of the shadow of death, He will stand by you till you reach the other side; He will stand by you in the dark night, and will never leave you, never forsake you. It is sweet to have Him to speak to; and though insensible of everything else around us, not insensible of His presence; He will make us know Himself.

I used to wonder also why the rod and staff are there: *"Thy rod and Thy staff, they comfort me."* I once heard it said that they were kept to beat the sheep with. Well, the crook at the end of the staff is to draw the sheep out of the ditches when in the wilderness; but, here in the valley of the shadow of death, they are with the Master, and talking to Him. The reason why they get into the ditches when in the wilderness is, that they are trying to get away from the Shepherd; but the Lord Jesus does not need to beat them, nor pull His own out of the ditches when near to Himself. His purpose is to protect and to defend us. The next verse tells us that there are enemies there (v. 5), but we have not a defenseless Shepherd; we have one with a rod and a staff in His hand, not to beat His sheep, but to put away His and their enemies—to make all clear for you and me, passing through the valley.

Notice, further, it is a **valley**. You know it is hard work climbing a hill-side sometimes; but how very easy it is to go down a valley! And, thank God, it is down the valley we have to go. He has made it easy for us.

We must also noticed that little word, **through**. We walk through the valley of the shadow of death—right through it. We do not stay there. I do not need to care when sometimes, in a train, I enter a tunnel, because I know we shall soon be out in the daylight; it may be dark and gloomy for a little while, but soon there is light and sunshine. And in the valley it cannot be dark when the Master is there, the Good Shepherd, for He is *"the light of the world."*

Another word is very sweet to me, and that is the word **walk**. It means He is in no hurry; we are going to walk through. And there is another cheering thought. You may carry a dead sheep, but it must be a living sheep that can walk through the valley. Well, here we read, *"Yea, though I walk through the valley of the shadow of death."* Then the next verse tells us He is going to feed us. We are not to be hungry there. I will tell you what workers need all through this weary world—we need feeding. We need feeding to give us strength; and the Lord Jesus, the Good Shepherd, knew that. He says, "I will feed you." He brings us to the valley, and what is He going to do? He spreads a table before us in the presence of our foes, and even Satan himself shall see us satisfied. Thank God for such a Shepherd, and such a Saviour!

Then this verse concludes by saying He is going to anoint us. You know Moses anointed the priests just before they went into the holy presence; the last thing was to put sweet savour on them. And so it will be with us. There is to be sweet savour put on us before we go into God's presence, and the Shepherd Himself is going to anoint us. He is the Good Shepherd, and giveth His life for the sheep.

I need not call your attention to that last verse—the Shepherd leads, and goodness and mercy bring up the rear; so that if a poor sheep does go astray, or get tired and lag behind, goodness and mercy come along and help the worn out one; the Shepherd goes first, and goodness and mercy follow after.

Now let us turn to John 10. Look at the 27th verse: *"My sheep hear My voice, and I know them, and they follow Me."*

Is there not something very sweet there? My friend, if you want to know the mark of true sheep, they follow the Shepherd; that is the mark of Christ's sheep – they know the Shepherd's voice, and go where He leads. Do we not get the Shepherd's voice in this blessed Book? Sometimes we get like Peter, and follow at a distance; but you know that is a bad place to be, at a distance. Sheep are known by following close to the Good Shepherd.

Some time ago, when dear Mr. Sankey and myself were in Chicago, a missionary arrived from Syria, and a friend said to him, "Do the shepherds all bring their sheep to the water at once?" "Yes, they bring them down for refreshment." And that is how I think the sheep gather together to feed on the Word; they come together for refreshment, and you know not what they are, except that they are Christ's sheep. But when the sheep have finished, they all follow their own shepherd.

Well, my friend asked if they ever refused to follow the shepherd. "Yes, sometimes a sheep gets sick, and then he will not follow." Now, I want to be charitable to every one. I used to see Christians doing what I thought was not right, and I said, "Why, they are surely not Christians." But now I think every man should be taken at his word; and if he makes a profession of faith in Christ Jesus, I believe him. When we see such an one doing what is not becoming of a Christian, going apparently over to the world, do not say he is not a sheep—that may be wrong, but say he is a sick sheep, that he is not healthy, and sick sheep go their own ways, and after their own hearts, too. Healthy sheep are known by following the shepherd: *"My sheep hear My voice, and I know them, and they follow Me."* Now, did you ever see a sick one? It is a sad thing to see a sick sheep in the flock. You know that very often there is a very bad disease among sheep—the foot-and-mouth disease; and these two parts are always diseased together. The disorder breaks out in the foot, and then soon after it appears in the mouth. Well, when a Christian visits you, and by-and-by begins to talk of Brother So-and-so, and commences to tell you something about him, you just get as far away as you can from that one. He has not been walking in fellowship with the Lord; he has the foot-and-mouth disease, and it is very catching; get away from him. The Lord does not want His sheep to be sick, but to be well and healthy.

Now look at the little word *"I know."* It has been one of the greatest comforts to me of any word in this blessed

Book. *"I know them."* My friends, you might pass through the busy streets of New York, and they could not tell you were a Christian; you would not perhaps see any one you know, or get a kind word. The first time I went to New York I was walking in Broadway; and there were thousands of people passing along that thoroughfare, but not one knew me, and I felt utterly lonely there. How sweet a thing it is for us to understand, that, though the world may not know us, yet Christ says, *"I know"* you—the Shepherd knows His sheep.

In Manchester, where I came from, we have what we call our "annual festivities" in Whitsun week; every Whitsun week the schools march in procession to some place appointed, but Whit Monday is the great day; the scholars of the Episcopal schools go out on that occasion. Two years ago there was a poor woman standing in the street; on one side she had one little girl by the hand, and on the other she had another little girl. By-and-by the procession came along, and they could not see at all, because of the crowd between them and the scholars. The woman pushed forward, and asked some men to let the girls stand in front and they could see over them; the men good-naturedly said, "Yes, and you can stand in front as well, if you like." Well, on the scholars came, and the first school passed and another, and yet another. The mother did not seem to look at one of them; she had her eyes fixed right on the distance, and did not seem to see these schools. By-and-by they heard the sound of the fifes and drums of the Industrial School: as soon as ever she heard that, she turned and said, "Willie's coming." The band came up, and the elder boys passed, but the mother did not seem to mind them; but when the little fellows came, in corduroy clothes, she looked eagerly among them, and soon cried, "Willie! Willie!" In a moment the boy sprang out of the ranks, and she clasped him in her arms and kissed him; she gave him a penny and an orange, and he went on again in his place in the procession. She knew him in that vast crowd, and loved him; when he passed, there was one eye saw him, and one heart loved him; she knew her boy, and she cared for her boy. Well, the Good Shepherd cares for us. He knows us and loves us, and He says, *"My sheep hear My voice, I know them, and they follow Me."* I tell you, friends, the more you and I know the Good Shepherd, the more closely do we follow Him; and the more do we love Him, because we understand better His mighty love to us.

I will ask you to turn to 1 Samuel 17. There we find a little illustration of what the Lord Jesus says—*"My sheep shall never perish."* Look at verses 33 to 37: now we get two different beasts here coming against the sheep, a lion and a bear; and we find David killed them both on purpose to deliver the innocent lamb from their grasp; the shepherd went out to rescue the innocent lamb. Now, what does this teach us? There is no animal as strong as the lion, and Satan is a roaring lion; yet one thing the lion can not do, it cannot use craft. But those who know tell us the craftiest thing on earth is a bear—the bear can go anywhere. The lion cannot climb a tree; the bear can. This, then, teaches the power of Satan; the lion and the bear—strength and cunning. Some people are always talking about their wonderful experience, they have got so high; but, however high you have got, the bear can follow; he can climb after you. The strength of the lion and the craft of the bear took off with the lamb, but David was a match for them both, and our Shepherd is a match both for the power of the devil and the craft of the devil; and neither the strength nor the wiles of Satan can get the lamb out of the Shepherd's flock.

Now turn to Luke 15:3-7. It is the parable we love to sing about—"The Ninety and Nine."

> *"And Jesus spake this parable unto them, saying: 'What man of you, having a hundred sheep, if he lose one of them, doth not leave the ninety and nine in the wilderness, and go after that which is lost, until he find it? And when he hath found it, he layeth it on his shoulders, rejoicing. And when he cometh home, he calleth together his friends and neighbours, saying unto them, "Rejoice with me, for I found my sheep which was lost." I say unto you, that likewise joy shall be in heaven over one sinner that repenteth, more than over ninety and nine just persons which need no repentance.'"*

I think we may get tired of this parable as soon as of that song, because it is just the parable put into verse. The shepherd went after this one sheep out of the ninety and nine. Is that not just the Good Shepherd coming after you and me, when we have gone astray? We have wandered, and He puts us on His shoulders. Have you ever observed that word "shoulders" – not shoulder, but shoulders? That poor sheep wants carrying; both shoulders are used for the sheep; and yet we find in Isaiah that one shoulder is enough to support the universe. Why did not he take the sheep to the ninety and nine instead of home? They would say, "Look at your wool, it's all torn and dirty"; and that sheep would have wandered away again as fast as possible; but when we understand the Shepherd's love and care, we cannot go astray.

I must ask you to turn once again with me to Isaiah 60:11. *"He shall feed His flock like a shepherd: He shall gather the lambs with His arm, and carry them in His bosom, and shall gently lead those that are with-young."*

This is a very sweet passage. You notice here that God promises to carry the lambs *"in His bosom"*; when He brought back the wandering sheep, it was *"on His shoulders."* I am thankful it was not a lamb that went astray. A great many people are afraid of young converts; well, Scripture says the old converts go astray as well as the young. You remember when the Lord Jesus Christ was here on earth, mothers brought the little ones to Him, and He took them in His arms and blessed them. The only ones He promises to take in His bosom here are the young ones—the lambs. It is for a purpose. He says He shall gently lead the mother with the young; He carries the lambs—why? For the purpose of helping the mother sheep. Do you not think it is very true that sometimes the sheep go astray? The world is attractive, and vanity, like a beautiful bubble, is attractive; but the Lord, I doubt not, will bring the sheep back; I believe if we do not come back, He will carry us back by main force—He will compel us to return.

Some time ago I went down to see some friends in the country; there were all the sheep and lambs in the fields. I thought, would it not be nice to imitate the Eastern shepherds, and have the sheep come after me? So I began to try to coax one as I would a dog. She would not mind me a bit, and my friend said, "You do not know about sheep, else you would never try to get that sheep to run after you." However, I still kept on; I ran after the sheep, and caught one of its lambs, and carried it; but the sheep did not come after me; it had a lamb still. I gave the lamb I had caught to my friend, and went after the second one, and, having caught it, I put a lamb under each arm. Well, you should have seen the sheep then. Why, she fixed her eyes on me, and kept as close to me as possible. When I walked, she walked; and when I ran, she ran. But I did not want her lambs, and so I just gave them back to her.

Now, there is a man going to business; he takes down the Bible, and, thinking all the time of his business, reads a portion. At night he has no time, because of business; he has got some big orders, or is expecting them. But he has one little girl, who is the light and life of the whole house, and her heart is full of joy; every time her father comes home, she runs to meet him. One day he does not meet her, and learns that his little darling is sick; she has caught that terrible disease, diphtheria. The doctor comes. "Can you do anything for my child?" "I will do my best," he says. But by-and-by the doctor says she is dying. The father comes to gaze on the sweet face, and puts his arms around his child. What would he not give to make her better?—his means, his business, his all. What are "foreign orders" now? What is his bank book now? He would give all he has in the world to make that child well. She looks at him as much as to say, "Father, won't you meet me in heaven?" And that child dies, and is carried to the cemetery and buried; and the father goes and puts flowers over her grave. But is she there? No, father; no, mother; your little child is not there. Why are you sad? She has gone home to the Father. It is **home** up there; and He wants you to know it is all *"vanity and vexation of spirit"* here. The Good Shepherd wants you to follow Him; He has laid down His life for the sheep.

Oh, my friends, do not follow the world, or the teachings of your own heart! Follow the Good Shepherd, keep close by

His side, and then He will lead you by green pastures and still waters, and make you to love to serve Him as never before. May God by His Holy Spirit endear that Shepherd to us more and more, for His own name's sake! Amen.

The Lamb of God

"Behold the Lamb of God!" (John 1:29).

We will turn to a few passages of Scripture, which, I trust, will fill our hearts with joy, bearing, as they do, on a subject of which the Scripture speaks more than any other – that is, **the Lord Jesus Christ as the Lamb of God**.

The first passage is in Exodus 12, and that is the first place in the Bible where we read about the death of the Lamb. In the 4th chapter of the Book of Genesis, we read that Abel *"brought the firstlings of the flock,"* but the word **lamb** is not mentioned. And in Genesis 22, we read that Isaac said to his father, as they were ascending Mount Moriah, *"Where is the lamb for a burnt offering?"* But we know that at the top of the mount it was not a lamb, but a ram, that was offered. Therefore the first place we read of the death of the lamb, as a sacrifice, is in our passage, Exodus 12; and here there cannot be the slightest doubt that it represents the Lord Jesus Christ, for Paul tells us that *"Christ our Passover is sacrificed for us."* Now, this is a chapter that has been frequently expounded, and I do not mean to enter upon it, but merely to point out one or two beautiful facts; for there is always something fresh to be gathered from God's Word.

In the first place there must have been at least two hundred and fifty thousand lambs slain that night, and yet we never find the word **lambs**; the word is always in the singular, and never in the plural. And when God appoints the killing of these lambs, He does not say kill **them**, but *"kill **it** in the evening."* It is as though God would see in them all but one lamb,

One Grand Presentation of His spotless Lamb.

All through, it is **the** lamb which is spoken of, and it is the Lamb of God that is pointed to.

Again, (vv. 21-23):

"Then Moses called for all the elders of Israel, and said unto

them, 'Draw out, and take you a lamb according to your families, and kill the Passover. And ye shall take a bunch of hyssop, and dip it in the blood that is in the basin, and strike the lintel and the two side-posts with the blood that is in the basin; and none of you shall go out at the door of his house until the morning. For the LORD will pass through to smite the Egyptians; and when He seeth the blood upon the lintel and on the two side-posts, the LORD will pass over the door, and will not suffer the Destroyer to come in unto your houses to smite you.'"

If you read that chapter very carefully, you will find that it was not an angel who was sent to destroy the Egyptians; but that the Lord Himself—JEHOVAH—went round to smite the Egyptians, and all the families where the blood was not found. At other times, when it was merely a question of destroying the enemy, (as in the camp of the Assyrians), we read that God sent an angel; but here, when it was a question of the safety of His own people, it appears as if the Lord could not trust an angel, but must come Himself. Again and again in the chapter we read that if was the Lord, and not an angel at all.

Then, with what was the blood to be sprinkled upon the door-posts and lintels? It was with hyssop. I believe that this has a meaning, though some may not agree with me here. The Bible tells us that Solomon *"spake of trees, from the cedar tree that is in Lebanon, even unto the hyssop that springeth out of the wall."* Every one knows that the cedar signifies pride, and magnificence; and so, on the same principle, the hyssop signifies humility and lowliness. Pride and the blood never go together. Wherever we see pride of heart, we may be sure that the blood is not there.

Picture of Substitution

"And every firstling of an ass thou shalt redeem with a lamb; and if thou wilt not redeem it, then thou shalt break his neck: and all the first-born of man among thy children shalt thou redeem" (Ex. 13:13).

We at once notice what a powerful picture we have here of substitution. Here is an unclean beast, an ass. As soon as it is born, it is sentenced to die; nothing can save it but substitution. Many tell us we do not need substitution; all we want is to have the mind developed. Well, you might develop the mind of that ass as much as you please, but no matter; unless it is redeemed, its neck must be broken. Man is in the same catalogue. You may educate him as much as you like; but unless he finds a substitute, unless he is born again, he cannot see the kingdom of God.

The Gospel Plan

> *"And unto the children of Israel thou shalt speak, saying 'Take ye a kid of the goats for a sin offering; and a calf and a lamb, both of the first year, without blemish, for a burnt-offering; also a bullock and a ram for peace-offerings, to sacrifice before the Lord: and a meat-offering mingled with oil; for today the Lord will appear unto you."*

Here we have the whole plan of Christianity brought out with great clearness. First, the Israelites were to bring a sin offering; then a burnt offering; thirdly, a peace offering; and lastly, a meat offering.

Here we have the Gospel plan. The first thing we have to do is to deal with Christ as the Sin-bearer. The Lord Jesus Christ has died for us, and there is our Sin offering. But when we have come to this, we are not done with Christ, or with Christianity; it is but the beginning of it, not the end. What is next? The burnt offering. What is that? Something placed on the alter, given to God, and never to be taken back. Something which God had said should be given to Him, and something burnt on the alter inside the tabernacle – not as was the case with the sin offering, outside the gate. What does it mean? Consecration.

What does God ask of me? Having put my sin away, He expects a consecrated life. Not saved because consecrated, but consecrated because saved. *"I beseech you, therefore, brethren, by the mercies of God, that ye present your bodies a living sacrifice, holy, acceptable unto God, which is your reasonable service"* (Rom. 12:1). It is not only our souls, but our bodies also. It is not, "I have such a glow of feeling here." That is not consecration. It is that every saved man and every saved woman should be wholly yielded to God, and ready to bear troubles and trials as the Master bore them. It is that our hands and our feet should be consecrated and used for the Master. It is that our tongues should be used for Him. It is not enough to say that "we are consecrated in spirit." God says, "I want your bodies."

But then that is not all. After the burnt offering comes the peace offering. The man and the woman who has got the peace of God is the man and the woman who is consecrated. It is only such who have God's peace, the peace of God.

Then comes the meat offering; and what does that imply? It is feasting on the Lamb of God. Why is it that a great many Christians prefer the newspaper to the Bible? Because they have not offered the burnt offering, they are not consecrated; because they have not the peace offering, and know not the peace of God: therefore, they do not enjoy the Scriptures. Sin put away, the body consecrated, the peace of God realized, then they may feed on the Lamb of God, as revealed in His precious Word. The reason why many do not enjoy feeding on the Bread of Life is that they have a bad conscience. They are nursing some secret sin, they are not consecrated to God, and therefore they do not enjoy His Word of Truth.

The Great Enemy

> *"And when the Philistines heard that the children of Israel were gathered together to Mizpeh, the lords of the Philistines went up against Israel. And when the children of Israel heard it, they were afraid of the Philistines. And the children of Israel said to Samuel, 'Cease not to cry unto the* Lord *our God for us, that He will save us out of the hand of the Philistines.' And Samuel took a sucking lamb, and offered it for a burnt-offering wholly unto the* Lord*; and Samuel cried unto the* Lord *for Israel; and*

> *the* L*ORD* *heard him. And as Samuel was offering up the burnt-offering, the Philistines drew near to battle against Israel, but the* L*ORD* *thundered with a great thunder on that day upon the Philistines, and discomfited them; and they were smitten before Israel"* (1 Sam. 7:7-10).

The Israelites had learned one useful lesson, and that was to be afraid of the Philistines. One of the first lessons for an individual, or for a church, is for that individual or church to learn to fear the enemy, Satan. There is terrible danger in the tendency of many to ignore Satan. A lady said to me the other day, "You are not so foolish as to believe in a personal devil?" "Oh, yes," I replied, "I am." "Why so?" "For the same reason that I believe in a personal Christ—because the Book tells me of both, and the Book cannot lie." What is written is enough for me. We have in these days songs about Satan, as if he was a myth; and we hear men shouting on the very streets about him. Nothing Satan likes so much as that; he just wants people to doubt his existence. The men who sing so lightly about him do not know much of his terrifying power.

Satan hates the church just as he hated Christ; and he would fain do to the church as he did to the Master. We must learn to dread him and avoid him. "Oh," said a man the other night, "I have had a fight with the devil!" "Did he conquer you?" "No; I was a match for him!" I tell you, the whole church of God is not a match for the old adversary. We want the power of Christ! We must trust a personal Christ to fight for us. I once learned a lesson from a little boy. He was quarrelling with a big boy, and the big one hit him. The little boy said, "It's no use my trying to fight thee; thou art too big for me. Just wait here till I fetch father, and he'll thrash thee." The big boy did not wait. But let us learn the lesson. It is no use our trying to fight Satan; let us go down on our knees, and pray for help from God, and Satan will not wait for that.

The Lamb Offered

Now, these Israelites were afraid, and they sought help

from God. They went to Samuel, and what did he do? He *"took a sucking lamb, and offered it for a burnt offering wholly unto the Lord."* The whole lamb was there. The lesson for us is to take the whole Lamb of God—Jesus, the Christ, the Son of God, the Son of man—as ours, with all His resources. The Philistines said, "We are not afraid of your sucking lamb. We have you in captivity: we will destroy you." But God thundered on the Philistines, and discomfited them. There was more power in that lamb, when offered to God, than in all the mighty hosts of the Philistines put together.

Many think that we want some wonderful gift before we can serve God; but what we do want is faith to trust Him, and then to go out and preach the simple Gospel, the story of the love of Christ. The man who preaches Christ will draw men to listen to him. The Christ of the Bible is still the mighty power. Men tell us we do not want the Bible now-a-days. If ever there was a time when we did want it, it is now. Honour the Bible in your preaching, and God will honour you. I have been about a good deal, but I have never known a man converted to God—I have known men converted to this or that religion, but never to God—apart from that blessed Book.

So the Israelites sacrificed a lamb, trusted in God and they were saved; and that is still the only secret of our safety from the enemy.

There is a great deal more about the Lamb in the Old Testament; and we might refer to many very interesting passages; but we must now pass on to the New Testament; and I will not touch upon the passages in the Gospel of John, the Acts of the Apostles, or the Epistle of Peter, but proceed to the closing book of the Bible.

> *"And I saw in the right hand of Him that sat on the throne a book written within and on the backside, sealed with seven seals. And I saw a strong angel proclaiming with a loud voice, 'Who is worthy to open the book, and to loose the seals thereof?' And no man in heaven, nor in earth, neither under the earth, was able to open the book, neither*

> *to look thereon. And I wept much, because no man was found worthy to open and to read the book, neither to look thereon. And one of the elders saith unto me, 'Weep not; behold, the Lion of the tribe of Judah, the Root of David, hath prevailed to open the book, and to loose the seven seals thereof.' And I beheld, and, lo, in the midst of the throne, and of the four beasts, and in the midst of the elders, stood a Lamb as it had been slain, having seven horns and seven eyes, which are the seven Spirits of God send forth into all the earth. And He came and took the book out of the right hand of Him that sat upon the throne. And when He had taken the book, the four beasts and four and twenty elders fell down before the Lamb, having every one of them harps, and golden vials full of odours, which are the prayers of the saints"* (Rev. 5:1-8).

There is something very wonderful about this scene in heaven, because it is the first time we read of the Lamb of God in the book of Revelation. The last time we read of Him was on the cross, in his sufferings and humiliation; that was where **man** put Him, but now look where **God** has put Him! Man nailed Him to the cross of shame; God set Him on the throne of glory. Man had despised and rejected Him; but now everybody praises Him, because they know His value.

Now notice that when John got up there, he began to weep. It is a strange thing, because it is the only time we read of tears of sorrow being shed in heaven. I believe that they were really tears of sorrow, although caused by mistake which he made. The question is asked: *"Who is worthy to take the book, and open the seals thereof?"* There is at first no response. John looked around, and saw no one come forward. People have right thoughts of themselves up yonder. There is not one in that shining throng, not one in the hosts of the redeemed, who thinks himself worthy. He looked around heaven—not one there; he looked on earth—not one there; he looked under the earth, and certainly he saw none there who could open the book. John wept; but one of the elders said, *"Weep not. This is not a place for sorrow; it is a place of rejoicing."* There are no tears of sorrow in heaven. *"God shall wipe away tears from their eyes"* (Rev. 7:17).

Doubtless there are tears of joy. Those who have crossed the Atlantic have seen many such. Here are a young gentleman and his wife. They have been some years abroad; they are now coming home. As the steamer approaches the harbour, they are talking much about the dear ones—wondering if mother will be altered much, and if father will be at the pier to meet them, and how their sisters are. By-and-by we enter the river; the tender comes puffing up alongside. They are getting nearer now, and you notice that they have no eyes for the fine scenery, or the bustling passengers. They are absorbed in watching for the pier. The young wife gets hold of the glass, and looks through it earnestly. "No; I can't see any one yet," she says. They get nearer and nearer. Up with the glass again—"I think I see some one like mother." The tender reaches the landing stage; there is a great crowd, but soon she sees "mother," and as she flings herself in her arms, there is a burst of tears. "Mother! Mother!" Are those tears of sorrow? Nay; but of wondrous joy. Is it not a little picture of what it may be when we get "home at last"? Do you not think that when we get to the pearly gates, and see the blessed Master waiting to receive us—see the wondrous Lamb of God, who took away our sins, ready to welcome us—there will be some such tears—weeping, for fullness of joy? Such are the only tear that shall be shed "in that bright world above."

But John was weeping for sorrow, and so the elder says, "Why, you have not looked in the right place, John!" "I have looked on the cherubim, I have looked among the twenty-four elders, I have looked amongst the multitudes of angels and of saints, I have looked on the earth; but among them all there is no one worthy to take and open the book!" "True, John; but you have not looked on the throne." He looks, and there are no more tears. The Lamb of God is worthy! On earth He was reckoned worthy of death, while there He is worthy of the throne, and the only one worthy to open the book. So our first glimpse of the Lamb in the book of Revelation reveals Him on the throne of glory.

Following and Praising

Now let us turn to Revelation 7:13-17, where we get another glimpse of the Lamb of God.

> *"And one of the elders answered, saying unto me, 'What are these which are arrayed in white robes, and whence came they?' And I said unto him, 'Sir, thou knowest.' And he said to me, 'These are they which came out of great tribulation, and have washed their robes, and made them white in the blood of the Lamb. Therefore they are before the throne of God, and serve Him day and night in His temple: and He that sitteth on the throne shall dwell among them. They shall hunger no more, neither thirst any more; neither shall the sun light on them, nor any heat. For the Lamb which is in the midst of the throne shall feed them, and shall lead them unto living fountains of waters; and God shall wipe away all tears from their eyes.'"*

The Lamb of God in the midst of His redeemed host! And notice that He *"shall feed them, and lead them unto living fountains."* He only does in heaven what He does for His own on earth.

> *"The Lord is my Shepherd, I shall not want. He maketh me to lie down in green pastures, He leadeth me beside the still waters"* (Ps. 23:1-2).

He satisfies us down here, and leads us; and He will satisfy us and lead is in heaven as well as on earth.

"They overcame him [the Devil] *by the blood of the Lamb, and by the work of their testimony; and they loved not their lives unto death"* (Rev. 12:11). The blood of the Lamb is the secret of their conquering strength.

> *"And I looked, and, lo, a Lamb stood on the Mount Sion, and with Him a hundred forty and four thousand, having His Father's name written in their forehands, and I heard a voice from heaven, as the voice of many water, and as the voice of a great thunder; and I heard the voice*

> *of harpers harping with their harps. And they sung as it were a new song before the throne, and before the four beasts, and the elders; and no man could learn that song by the hundred and forty and four thousand, which were redeemed from the earth. These are they which were not defiled with women; for they are virgins. They are they which follow the Lamb whithersoever He goeth. These were redeemed from among men, being the first fruits unto God and to the Lamb. And in their mouth was found no guile; for they are without fault before the throne of God"* (Rev. 14:1-5).

"His Father's name written on their foreheads"! There is something very suggestive about this expression. We read in the 13th chapter that the mark of the beast might be placed on the brow or on the right hand. It seems that some people might not like to have the mark blazoned on their foreheads, and so the beast permits them to put his mark on the palm of the right hand, where it might be hidden. But the Father's name must be blazoned on their forehead. It is not enough, then, to see that the mark of the beast is not on the brow, for it may be covered up in the hand; what we want is to see that the Father's name is stamped on the brow. He will not have any one ashamed of Him or of His mark. If we have it at all, it must be displayed on the brow, where it can be seen by all. There is one thing more about a mark on the brow, and that is that the man who bears it is the only one who does not see it. So, when a man is wholly consecrated to God, he is the last one to talk about it. His fellow-disciples will see it, the world around will see it; but when a man himself finds it out, and talks about it, very few people can see it.

Fighting and Conquering

> *"And they sing the song of Moses the servant of God, and the song of the Lamb, saying 'Great and marvellous are Thy works, Lord God Almighty; just and true are Thy ways, Thou King of saints. Who shall not fear Thee, O Lord, and glorify Thy name? For Thou only art holy; for*

> *all nations shall come and worship before Thee, for Thy judgements are made manifest.'" ... "These shall make war with the Lamb, and the Lamb shall overcome them: for He is Lord of lords and King of kings; and they that are with Him are called, and chosen, and faithful"* (Rev. 15:3-4, 17:14).

I have quoted these passages because it is just the course of those who follow the Lamb. First of all, they are not ashamed of Him; and then they follow Him; and as they follow Him they sing "the song of the Lamb." Nobody ever sings from the heart but they who follow the Lamb of God, and who have been redeemed by His blood. Then, as they sing, they fight; and as they fight they conquer. But how do they fight? The Lamb goes first and slays the enemies, and gives them the credit. Even as God thundered on the Philistines, and smote them, and then gave Israel the credit for discomfiting them, so it is confessing, following, praising, fighting, conquering, and all with the Lamb of God, and by the Lamb of God.

In Revelation 21:9, we find they finish up—as every one likes to finish his day's work—with a supper: *"Blessed are they which are called unto the marriage supper of the Lamb."*

Now, this supper is the last meal of the day. After breakfast, we go out to work, after dinner we have work again, but after supper we do not expect work—it is rest. So, after the marriage supper of the Lamb, there lies before us God's grand eternal rest. The weary pilgrimage is past, the hard fight is over, the victory is won, and the rest has come. Truly they are blessed who shall sit down to that supper; and how thankful we should be that the Bible tells us of this supper!

> There all His people eternally dwell
> With Him who hath let them so safely and well;
> The toilsome way over, the wilderness past,
> And Canaan the blessed is theirs at the last.

> *"And I saw no temple therein: for the Lord God Almighty and the Lamb are the temple of it. And the city had no need of the sun, neither of the moon, to shine in it: for the glory of God did lighten it, and the Lamb is the light thereof. And the nation of them which are saved shall walk in the light of it; and the kings of the earth do bring their glory and honour into it. And the gates of it shall not be shut all day: for there shall be no night there. And they shall bring the glory and honour of the nations into it. And there shall in no wise enter into it anything that defileth, neither whatsoever workth abomination, or maketh a lie, but they which are written in the Lamb's Book of Life ... And there shall be no more curse: servants shall serve Him; and they shall see His face; and His name shall be in their foreheads"* (Rev. 21:22-27, 22:3-4).

That is the last place in the Bible that we read of the Lamb. He is on the throne, and His servants serve Him, while their greatest delight is to see His face. We have seen where man put the Lamb of God, and we have seen where God the Father has put Him—man put Him on the cross, God put Him on the throne. First there was suffering, then glory. And that is the rule for us, His people—first the cross, then the crown. But, above all, there was for Him but one way to that grand mediatorial throne, and that way lay by the cross. Thus we see the Lamb of God suffering on the cross, and then crowned in glory. *"Wherefore God also hath highly exalted Him, and given Him a name which is above every name; that at the name of Jesus every knee should bow, of things in heaven, and things in earth, and things under the earth; and that every tongue should confess that Jesus Christ is Lord, to the glory of God the Father"* (Phil. 2:9-11).

> Lamb of God, our souls adore Thee,
> While upon Thy face we gaze;
> There the Father's love and glory
> Shine in all their brightest rays!
> Oh, what wonderous love and mercy!

Thou didst lay Thy glory by,
And for us didst come from heaven,
As the Lamb of God, to die!

Lord, we learn, with hearts adoring,
Wondrous love in Thy shed blood!
Glory, glory everlasting
Be to Thee, Thou Lamb of God!

Law and Grace

"The law was given by Moses, but grace and truth came by Jesus Christ" (John 1:17).

In considering this subject, I want to look at the contrast which we find between the life of Moses and that of our blessed Saviour.

I am quite aware that in many things Moses can be taken as a contrast to Him. I think, in fact, that much in the Bible can be taken as a contrast to Christ, as well as a type.

For instance, we read of Abel being a shepherd; and we read of Christ being our Shepherd, and therefore Abel is a type of Christ; yet there is a marked contrast. In the one case the sheep died for the shepherd, as when Abel offered of the firstlings of his flock unto the Lord; and in the other case it was the Shepherd who died for the sheep. Abel, then, is a type of Christ, he can also in certain instances be taken as a contrast to the Lord Jesus Christ.

And so all through this blessed book we find that Moses and Christ can be taken in contrast one to the other. In contrast, yet not antagonistic; just as law and grace are in contrast to one another, and yet not by any means antagonistic; because the One who manifested His grace gave the law, and the One who gave His Son Jesus Christ to be the Saviour gave Moses to the people.

So, bearing this in mind, let us turn to the Bible—which can always vindicate itself—and find what it teaches. I might say a great deal with which you might not agree; but what the Scriptures say, you must believe, if you believe the Word to be of God.

Death by the Law—Life by Christ

Turn then to Exodus 2:11-12, where we find that the first public act of Moses which is recorded, is in connection with death: *"He slew the Egyptian, and hid him in the sand."* That was his first public act recorded in this book. As soon as he had gone out and observed an Egyptian smiting one of his brethren, he slew the Egyptian.

Look now at the life of Christ. We find that one of the first things in connection with the public life of Christ was giving life. The first public act of Moses was in connection with death, while one of the first—I will not say **the** first—public acts of the Lord Jesus Christ was to give life.

Servants – Sons

> *"And the angel of the LORD appeared unto him in a flame of fire out of the midst of a bush; and he looked, and behold, the bush burned with fire, and the bush was not consumed. And Moses said, 'I will now turn aside and see this great sight, why the bush is not burnt.' And when the LORD saw that he turned aside to see God, God called unto him out of the midst of the bush, and said, 'Moses, Moses.' And he said, 'Here I am.' And He said, 'Draw not nigh hither: put off thy shoes from off thy feet, for the place whereon thou standest is holy ground'"* (Ex. 3:2-5).

Here we find that Moses could not come near to God without taking his shoes off his feet. Why? Because no servant ever dared to come into the presence of his master with shoes on his feet; and therefore Moses, as the servant, is commanded to put his shoes from off his feet ere he drew near to God. Turn now to Luke 15. Here we see that the father runs to meet the poor returning prodigal, and his first words are:

> *"Bring forth the best robe, and put it on him; and put a ring on his hand, and shoes on his feet"* (v. 22).

Law says, "Put off thy shoes"; grace says, "Put them on." By the law we cannot come nigh to God; but by grace we can come nigh, or rather are **made nigh**. God, in grace, will have none without shoes on their feet as the token of their sonship.

The Serpent Manifested

> *"And Moses… said, 'But, behold, they will not believe me, nor hearken unto my voice: for they will say, "The Lord hath not appeared unto thee."' And the Lord said unto him, 'What is that in thine hand?' And he said, 'A rod.' And He said, 'Cast it on the ground.' And he cast it on the ground, and it became a serpent; and Moses fled from before it"* (Ex. 4:1-3).

This is the second time we read about the serpent in the Bible. The first time was in the garden of Eden; and now we read that in the presence of the Lord, the rod became a serpent. It is a type of the power of the law. God gave the law to manifest the serpent's power. The law cannot kill the serpent, only grace can; but the law manifests the presence of the serpent. This is what the law given by Moses is for.

Leprosy – Cleansing

Again, read at the 6th verse:

> *"Put now thine head into thy bosom. And he put his hand into his bosom; and when he took it out, behold, his hand was leprous as snow."*

This is the first place in the Bible where we read of leprosy. Moses wanted a sign, and God seems to have given him, as a sign, a picture of sin in his hand.

Thus, the law could only manifest the leprosy of sin; it is the blood of Christ which cleanseth. *"The law was given by Moses, but grace and truth came by Jesus Christ"* (John 1:17). And the first leper in the Bible was Moses himself, through whom the law was given.

Sorrow by the Law – Joy by Grace

Read, again, Exodus 8:19, where we find that, at the command of the Lord, Moses spake to Aaron, and he stretched forth his rod, and all the waters became blood. In connection, turn to John 2. It may be that these passages are as familiar to you as ABC, but all is fresh to the Christian's heart.

We find that at the marriage in Cana of Galilee, they wanted wine; and the mother of Jesus said to the servants: *"Whatsoever He saith unto you, do it."*

We are sometimes asked, what do you preach? Oh, if we preached like Mary, what good results might follow! It is a very short sermon, but none ever preached a better or safer one than that. *"Whatsoever He saith unto you, do it."* If there is any difficult matter, have a Bible reading about it; and when you find what He says, *"do it."* There would not be a single division in the Church of God today if we all listened to this sermon, and did it. Often we make mistakes, just because we are always arguing about these things instead of simply **doing them**.

Mark how the servants did the Saviour's command, without questioning, and the result was *"good wine."*

> *"This beginning of miracles did Jesus in Cana of Galilee, and manifested forth His glory; and His disciples believed on Him"* (v. 11).

Some have been greatly puzzled why the Lord Jesus Christ should have turned water into wine; but I believe that what He did was right—He could make no mistakes.

Mark, all the miracles that Christ ever did afterward were embraced in the first one. Water is ever the type of death and sorrow, while wine is the type of joy; and so the Lord Jesus Christ came to turn sorrow into joy. He gives, as is set forth in this miracle, plenty and joy, instead of poverty and sorrow. He makes our hearts to run right over. He has filled many a sad heart and made it glad. So it is ever with our Lord; for death, He gives life; for tears, joy; and for sorrow, gladness of heart. The first miracle that Moses did was to turn water into blood, the sign of death and sorrow; while the first miracle wrought by Jesus Christ was turning water into wine, the sign of joy.

Darkness – Light

> *"And Moses stretched forth his hand towards heaven; and there was a thick darkness in all the land of Egypt three days"* (Ex. 10:22).

Here, again, we see the law brings darkness. Now turn to John 9. Jesus, passing by, sees a man which was blind from his birth, and when his disciples inquired concerning it, Jesus told them why it was—that the works of God should be made manifest. *"I am the light of the world."* And spitting on the ground, He made clay and healed the man. Read also the closing verse of the preceding chapter:

> *"Then took they up stones to cast at Him; but Jesus hid Himself, and went out of the temple, going through the midst of them, and so passed by. And as Jesus passed by..."*

Those who divided the Bible into chapters have very often made these divisions in the wrong place. Here, as in many other places, the very point is lost by the division. They would have stoned Him, but He hid Himself from them, but goes right to the poor beggar. He was hid from the Jews, but at the very first case of need He revealed Himself. He hid Himself from people with sight, but revealed Himself to people without sight. He hid Himself from the proud Pharisees, but revealed Himself to the blind beggar. So it is still; when we think we are all right and that we see, He is hid from us; but when we know that we are blind, then He gives a sight of Himself.

So we read that Moses brought darkness; but the Lord Jesus brought light. Even more, He was **the** Light, and darkness could not stand before Him.

> *"And it came to pass that at midnight the LORD smote all the firstborn in the land of Egypt, from the first born of Pharaoh that sat on his throne, unto the firstborn of the captive that was in the dungeon; and all the firstborn of*

> *cattle. And Pharaoh rose up in the night, he, and all his servants, and all the Egyptians; and there was a great cry in Egypt, for there was not a house where there was not one dead"* (Ex. 12:29-30).

The last scene in the land of Egypt was death. The first public act of Moses was in connection with death. Look now at the Lord Jesus Christ. His last public act was when He took the sinner's place in death—when He died that we might have life.

Thus, in connection with Moses we find blood, darkness and death; in connection with Jesus Christ we find wine, light and life. We find nothing in connection with the law but darkness, sorrow and death, the result of sin made manifest; but the moment we get from the law to grace, then it is light, joy and life, through the Lord Jesus Christ. Thus from all these Scriptures we see the strong contrast between the Lord Jesus Christ and Moses.

But again, in Exodus 19:16, we find that the giving of the law on the mount was with thundering, and lightnings, the noise of the trumpet, and the mountains smoking.

> *"Then answered Peter, and said unto Jesus, 'Lord, it is good for us to be here; if Thou wilt, let us make here three tabernacles—one for Thee, and one for Moses, and one for Elias.' While he yet spake, behold, a bright cloud overshadowed them; and behold a voice out of the cloud, which said, 'This is My beloved Son, in whom I am well pleased; hear ye Him!'"* (Matt. 17:4-5).

What a contrast! When the law was given by God Himself, it was with thundering, lightnings and darkness; but when Christ was manifested, it was with a bright cloud, and His face shining as the sun. When the law came, it was with darkness; but grace was with light.

No Stepping-stones to Christ

Again, in Exodus 20:24-26, we have a description given of

the alter which was to be built:

> *"An alter of earth thou shalt make unto Me, and shalt sacrifice thereon thy burnt-offerings, and thy peace-offerings, thy sheep, and thine oxen: in all places where I record My name I will come unto thee, and I will bless thee. And if thou wilt make Me an alter of stone, thou shalt not build it of hewn stone: for if thou lift up thy tool upon it, thou hast polluted it. Neither shalt thou go up by steps unto Mine alter, that thy nakedness be not discovered thereon."*

What makes these verses so striking is the fact that they are spoken just as soon as the law was given, and immediately after the ten commandments.

God had said, *"Do this and live"*; but He knew that he could not keep the law and get life, and so now He tells them how they may get life and get near Him. Having given the law, He speaks of building the altar upon which to make sin-offerings. But observe, the altar is to be built of earth; or, if of stone, it must not be hewn stone. It must be of the natural stone. *"Neither shalt thou go up by steps unto Mine altar."* As if God would not have us think that we may by ourselves rise, as it were, to meet Him. We think we must go up one and another step to meet God. Not so; He will not ask us to come a single step—**not one**. Grace just comes all the way from heaven, right to the feet of the lost, guilty sinner, and prays him to be saved, to accept eternal life. No sign, no worship, no fire is required of us, in order to be saved; nothing but acceptance.

We cannot get to heaven by works or merit, or anything we can do; but the very moment we take the lost, guilty sinner's place, God comes right to us and saves us, and brings us nigh unto Himself. He does it all.

"About Three Thousand"

But now turn to Exodus 32:26. After the sin of the people, Moses said: *"Who is on the LORD's side? Let him come unto me. All the sons of Levi gathered themselves together unto him."*

And having received His command, they went forth into the camp, slaying the people—*"And there fell of the people that day about three thousand men"* (v. 28). Notice the very expression—*"about three thousand."*

Turn now to Acts 2:41. After Peter had declared the Gospel, *"They that gladly received his Word were baptized; and the same day there were added to them about three thousand souls."* You observe the very same expression—*"about three thousand"* souls.

The very first time the law was preached, *"about three thousand"* were killed, and the very first time grace was preached, *"about three thousand"* were saved.

So all through the life of Moses and the life of Jesus Christ we get wonderful contrasts. But now let us go further.

Entering the Promised Land

> *"And Joshua said unto the people, 'Sanctify yourselves, for tomorrow the LORD will do wonders among you...' And the LORD said unto Joshua, 'This day will I begin to magnify thee in the sight of all Israel'"* (Josh. 3:5-7).

Observe that Joshua said first, *"The LORD will do wonders"*; and when the Lord spake, He said, *"I will magnify thee."* Joshua is to do the wonders. When men magnify God, God will magnify them.

But mark here, Moses, who represented the law, could not take the people **into** the promised land, although he brought them close to it—Joshua, who was a type of Christ, had to lead them into it. So, what can the law do? It can only show us the promised land. Grace it must be that leads us into it.

Read further; in the 14th-17th verses, we find that the Israelites passed over on dry ground.

> *"And it came to pass, when the people removed from their tents to pass over Jordan, and the priests bearing the ark of the covenant before the people; and as they that bare the ark were come unto Jordan, and the feet of the priests that*

bare the ark were dipped in the brim of water (for Jordan overfloweth all his banks all the time of harvest), that the waters which came down from above stood and rose up upon a heap very far from the city Adam, that is beside Zaretan: and those that came down toward the sea of the plain, even the Salt Sea, failed, and were cut off: and the people passed over right against Jericho. And the priests that bare the ark of the covenant of the LORD stood firm on dry ground in the midst of Jordan, and all the Israelites passed over on dry ground, until all the people passed clean over Jordan."

I used, when a boy, in reading that beautiful book, the *Pilgrim's Progress,* to imagine that I had to pass through the waters of death into Canaan. And when the minister preached, it sometimes took my breath away and chilled my very blood to hear him talk of the cold, icy Jordan, and of the Christian coming along and looking across to the golden city; and then entering the cold river. After a little he begins to cry out, the water is so cold, and when he gets deeper, he can scarce keep his feet, and at last when he gets to the middle of the river, the waves go over him, and he cries out, "Thy billows have gone over me," and he disappears. Now, there is no such thing in the Bible. When the Israelites went over the Jordan, remember, the priests bearing the ark went before the people, and as their feet were dipped in the brim of the water, the river stood back in a heap and the people passed over dry shod, while the priests with the ark stood in the midst till all had passed over. So, I expect to cross the river dry shod. The waters of Jordan will not touch us. The billows and waves have gone over the Master's head and will not go over ours.

In the 23rd Psalm we have a beautiful picture of it all: *"Though I walk through the valley of the shadow of death, I will fear no evil; for Thou art with me"* (v. 4). So it will be with us. It is but the **shadow** of death.

Remember, that it was night when the Israelites crossed the Red Sea; but when they crossed the river of Jordan, it was probably daylight. Just imagine the sun shining upon the waters standing up in a heap, and there you will have the picture, which, I believe, David had in his mind when he wrote this sentence. The shadow of the waters would be falling upon their path—and only the shadow!

Two more thoughts here. How did the Israelites get through the river? They went right across it. And so it was not walking **in** the valley, it is walking **through** it. Just as when a railroad train enters a dark tunnel; you do not expect to stop in the tunnel, but to get out into light on the other side.

But again: *"Though I walk through the valley."* We might carry a dead man through, but it takes a **live** man to walk. So we fear no death; with Christ at our side we walk through, and He will lead us to the bright land beyond.

What the Law Cannot Do

But now let us consider some things which the law cannot do for the sinner, but which grace can do.

In Acts 13:38-39, we read: *"Be it known unto you therefore, men and brethren, that through this Man is preached unto you the forgiveness of sins: and by Him all that believe are justified from all things from which ye could not be justified by the law of Moses."*

The law, therefore, cannot justify us, and, if we are to be justified, it must be by grace; and, if we are not justified, we are not saved.

Again, in Romans 8 (I was going to call it the Gospel of Romans, and surely that is the Gospel—*"No condemnation"*—good news, surely!):

> *"There is therefore now no condemnation to them which are in Christ Jesus, who walk not after the flesh, but after the Spirit. For the law of the Spirit of life in Christ Jesus has made me free from the law of sin and death. For what the law could not do, in that it was weak through the flesh, God sending His own Son in the likeness of sinful flesh, and for sin, condemned sin in the flesh."*

Here is something further that the law could not do. What is that? It could not make me free from the law of sin and death. Freedom—there is no slave here; whether on earth or in heaven, we are in Christ, and the law of Christ gives liberty. As the Lord Himself said, *"Ye shall know the truth, and the truth shall make you free"* (John 8:32). Every one who believes in that blessed Saviour, the Son of God, is a free man. He is free even now—as free as he will be in the land above.

The Broken Law

I find a difficulty in the minds of many in taking their place as guilty sinners. As a lady once said to me, "I cannot see that one who has broken one of the commandments can be as bad as another who has broken five, or another who has broken the whole ten laws." But I said, "Remember, God never gave five or ten laws; He only gave one, which consisted of ten commandments. Just look at that watch; if you were to count the wheels, you would find, perhaps, ten or more, yet it is just one watch. And further, if you break every wheel, it is of course, a broken watch and will not go. Yet, if you break only one wheel, it is still a broken watch, and will not go. So we have broken the law if we have broken a single command in the Book." Still the lady could not see it, and so I said, "Suppose you were hanging by a chain right over a precipice: that chain consists of ten links; and, if a man were to take a hammer and smash every link, where would you go?" "To the bottom of course."

"But suppose only one link is broken, where would you go?" "That would be just as bad; I would fall."

"So then, if you break one command, it is just as bad as breaking the whole law. *'He that offendeth in one point is guilty of all.'* No matter how good you are, still you have broken **one**, and down to the bottom you must go."

It just takes as much grace to save the best men in the world as to save the vilest. Nothing but grace can bring us forth—the law cannot give liberty, but grace gives it.

No Righteousness by the Law

> *"I do not frustrate the grace of God; for if righteousness come by the law, then Christ is dead in vain"* (Gal. 2:21).

These are very solemn words, for, if it be possible for righteousness to come to one man by the law, then it is possible for righteousness to come to every man, and *"Christ,"* then, says the Word, *"is dead in vain."*

> *"Is the law then against the promises of God? God forbid; for if there had been a law given which could have given life, verily righteousness should have been by the law"* (Gal. 3:21).

If it had been possible for the mighty God to have given law which should have given life—if it have been possible, then He would never have given a law of death. Therefore, we find that another thing which the law cannot do, is that it cannot give life.

The Law Cannot Make Perfect

> *"For the law made nothing perfect, but the bringing in of a better hope did; by the which we* ***draw nigh unto God****"* (Heb. 7:19).

The law can never bring us nigh unto God. We have thus seen four things which the law cannot do—it cannot justify, it cannot make me free, it cannot make me righteous and it cannot make me perfect.

Many do not believe in perfection; but if you are not perfect, you cannot go to heaven. But here we have the perfection: the One who gives me justification, freedom and righteousness, also gives me perfection. He makes me perfect by making me a partaker of His own holiness; and thus we are as perfect as the Master Himself, because He is everything **for** us and **to** us, if we will have Him.

The End of the Law

But if the law cannot save us, what did God give the law for? It is very plain, if you will turn to Romans 3:19:

> *"Now we know that what things soever the law saith, it saith to them who are under the law; that every mouth may be stopped, and all the world may become guilty before God."*

You say you never committed a murder; that you have been charitable, religious and good; that you have said your prayers, and so on; but remember, God did not give the law to make you talk about yourself – He gave the law to stop your mouth, not to open it. God did not give us the law and ten commandments to make us so good that He could save us, but to prove to us that we were so bad that our only course was to accept His salvation. If many could get rid of their own goodness, it would not be difficult to get rid of their badness. *"He is able."*

But I must first take my proper place as a sinner, and then I will see myself in Him. I just accept His salvation, that is all.

A New Creation Wanted

When I was going for a walk one day, I met a little girl with a jug in her hand, running on an errand for her mother. On the way, her foot tripped on a little stone, and down she went, and the jug was broken into more than fifty pieces. She began to cry, saying that her mother would punish her. Suppose, when I had got to her, she said, "Pick up the pieces, and get some of that cement which they sell, and put them together." Why, it would have been a broken jug still—all cracked and disfigured. People do not like cracked jugs. Well, I did not propose any such thing. I just said, "Don't you cry; come with me, and we'll get a new one." I took her to a shop and, after looking at five or six jugs, she selected one, and I paid the price, only a few coppers. "Now," I said, "are you afraid that your mother will be angry?" "Oh, no; it's a deal better than the one I broke."

Now, that is just like the righteousness of the law. A stumbling-block, it may be a very small one, is put in our path, and down we go, and all our righteousness is smashed to pieces. And Christ did not come all the way from heaven in order to pick up the pieces and put them together. No. The perfect righteousness of a perfect Saviour—a new creation and not the old one.

It is the law, therefore, that stops the mouth. We are convicted, and now Christ is our satisfaction. God says, "My Son's blood has been shed; believe on Him, and in Him you are justified, accepted, and made perfect." He is "made unto us wisdom, and righteousness, and sanctification and redemption." Everything is **in Him for us**.

The Grace of God that Bringeth Salvation

And now, one more passage:

> *"For the grace of God that bringeth salvation hath appeared to all men, teaching us that, denying ungodliness and worldly lusts, we should live soberly, righteously and godly, in this present age"* (Tit. 2:11-12).

I remember the first time I went to London, a Christian gentleman came to me, and said, "Henry Moorhouse, I want you to remember this, *'The grace of God that bringeth salvation, hath appeared to all men'*; but," he said, "you must not stop there; read on—teaching us to live as we choose, as being free from the commandments? No. It is just like this: God had set up a law, and men failed to come up to it; and now, instead of lowering His standard to our level, He has raised it higher and set it in heaven, and says, 'Come up to this.' The law says 'Do this!' but grace teaches me how to do it."

If men could not keep the law of Moses, how can Christians keep a law which is much higher? Let us remember that grace gives us strength, and teaches us, *"that denying ungodly and worldly lusts, we should live soberly, righteously and godly in this present world."*

Grace teaches us that we are not under the law, thank God!

But we are under grace. Grace gives us eternal life. Grace gives us a Master to serve, footprints to walk in, a Shepherd to lead us, and strength and power to follow the Shepherd, to serve the Master and walk in His blessed footsteps.

May God lead us to know that we are not under Moses, but under Christ—not under law, but under grace. And to His name be all glory!

www.ingramcontent.com/pod-product-compliance
Lightning Source LLC
LaVergne TN
LVHW010106110826
845155LV00028B/504

* 9 7 8 1 9 2 6 7 6 5 2 7 3 *